CALLED
TO
PREACH

CALLED TO PREACH

FULFILLING THE HIGH CALLING OF EXPOSITORY PREACHING

STEVEN J. LAWSON

BakerBooks

a division of Baker Publishing Group
Grand Rapids, Michigan

© 2022 by Steven J. Lawson

Published by Baker Books
a division of Baker Publishing Group
PO Box 6287, Grand Rapids, MI 49516-6287
www.bakerbooks.com

Printed in the United States of America

Library of Congress Cataloging-in-Publication Data
Names: Lawson, Steven J., author.
Title: Called to preach : fulfilling the high calling of expository preaching / Steven J. Lawson.
Description: Grand Rapids, MI : Baker Books, a division of Baker Publishing Group, [2022] | Includes bibliographical references.
Identifiers: LCCN 2021035424 | ISBN 9780801094866 (paperback) ISBN 9781540902467 (cloth) ISBN 9781493434060 (ebook)
Subjects: LCSH: Expository preaching.
Classification: LCC BV4211.3 .L385 2022 | DDC 251—dc23
LC record available at https://lccn.loc.gov/2021035424

Unless otherwise indicated, Greek and Hebrew terms and translations are from Walter Bauer, Frederick William Danker, William F. Arndt, and F. Wilbur Gingrich, *A Greek-English Lexicon of the New Testament and Other Early Christian Literature*, 3rd ed. (BDAG) (Chicago: University of Chicago Press, 2000).

Baker Publishing Group publications use paper produced from sustainable forestry practices and post-consumer waste whenever possible.

22   23   24   25   26   27   28   7   6   5   4   3   2   1

To Derek W. H. Thomas
Faithful friend,
Gifted preacher,
Brilliant theologian

CONTENTS

INTRODUCTION

In every generation, the church of Jesus Christ rises or falls with its pulpit. This statement meets few exceptions. No church, no denomination, no movement rises any higher than its proclamation of the word of God. The importance of preaching for the edification of believers and the evangelism of the lost cannot be overstated. Over the centuries, every history-altering era of church history has been defined by the strength of its preaching. And every spiritually low season has been marked by a famine in the land of hearing the word of the Lord.

When the pulpit is strong, the church is strengthened, and her witness to the world is fortified. But when the pulpit is weak, the church languishes in spiritual listlessness, and society suffers for it.

The modern-day church has largely forgotten this truth. Church leaders look to the secular marketplace for new ideas to revitalize the work of God. Endless pragmatic strategies attempt to resuscitate the church. But each worldly remedy is deficient in reaching the goal. The truth remains—that which is born of the flesh is flesh.

What is widely overlooked is that God established long ago the primary means of grace to be the preaching of His word. In both the Old and New Testaments, the chief method God has chosen to carry out His redemptive work is the Spirit-empowered proclamation of biblical truth. Nothing must ever be allowed to supplant the primacy of the pulpit—not if the church is to flourish.

Tragically, faithful preaching has become a forgotten science and a lost art. New ideas about preaching flood our conferences and podcasts. They promise church growth, numerical success, and personal fulfillment, yet minimize biblical exposition. They all fall woefully short of the permanent pattern set by God in Scripture. Only the centrality of preaching His word can accomplish the task. We cannot improve on what God has ordained.

Regardless of the whims of the times, the church is never allowed to redefine its mission nor its methods. We must never alter what God has fixed into place. No one is at liberty to invent new methods that rise above the pulpit. If the church is to be what Jesus Christ, the Head of the church—the master Architect—designed it to be, then it must follow His divine blueprint.

This book is a bold call to those summoned by Christ to preach the word. Strong preachers are needed in this desperate hour, those who understand the high call that has been placed upon their lives. Biblical preaching is the vibrant heartbeat that pumps spiritual life into the body of Christ. The Scripture rightly preached in the power of the Spirit will elevate worship and mature believers. And a biblical pulpit will mobilize Christians in the cause of gospel outreach, both locally and globally.

Truly, the church is strongest when the pulpit is strongest.

In the following pages, I will set before you what the Bible says about this lofty responsibility of expository preaching. This is not a book that presents brand-new solutions for the pulpit. Nor is it the result of surveying church attendees or unsaved neighbors about what they want to hear. To the contrary, this book is a serious look at Scripture itself and consults the giants of church history to answer questions such as: Who should preach? What should preaching look like? How should we prepare our sermons? How should we deliver them to honor God?

Having surveyed the landscape we will explore, let us now begin our journey.

Steven J. Lawson
Dallas

ONE

Divinely Summoned

DISCERNING THE CALL

The ministry is the most honorable employment in the world.
Jesus Christ has graced this calling by His entering into it.

Thomas Watson[1]

Preachers are not made—they are born. No seminary can make an expositor. No Bible college can create a preacher. No church can manufacture a man gifted in the pulpit. Only God can call a preacher. These individuals were chosen before time began for this sacred task.

To exposit the word is the most strategic assignment ever entrusted to any person. Granted, every vocational calling is God-ordained and is, of course, important. But this summons to preach carries the strictest accountability before

God. There can be no higher calling than to be a mouthpiece for God.

In his landmark book *Preaching and Preachers*, Dr. Martyn Lloyd-Jones addressed this high call of biblical preaching with penetrating insight. This famed expositor made his case for the primacy of the pulpit in his opening statement when he asserted, "The work of preaching is the highest and the greatest and the most glorious calling to which anyone can ever be called."[2] Lloyd-Jones underscored what the Bible establishes, that preaching the word is to be the primary means of grace in all ministry.

Lloyd-Jones added, "The most urgent need in the Christian church today is true preaching; and as it is the greatest and most urgent need in the church, it is obviously the greatest need of the world also."[3]

The Greatest Need

Lloyd-Jones's words are as relevant today as when he first wrote them. As the ministry of the word goes, so goes the church. And as the church goes, in turn, so goes much of the culture and the world. To revive the pulpit is to bring the strongest influence to bear upon the spiritual life of the church at the highest level. Ultimately, it will have the greatest repercussions on the world. The pulpit is *that* strategic.

This primacy of preaching was established long ago. Throughout the Old Testament, God sent faithful prophets to declare, "Thus says the LORD" (Exod. 4:22). Then God preceded the coming of the Messiah by sending a preacher to prepare His coming. John the Baptist was a voice in the wilderness, announcing the coming of the long-awaited anointed One (Matt. 3:3). When God sent His own Son into the world, He called Him to be a preacher (Isa. 49:1–2). No higher endorsement of preaching could be given than for the Son of Man to be called into this holy assignment.

Jesus Christ then called twelve disciples to preach (Matt. 10:7). He spent three years training them so that "repentance for forgiveness of sins would be proclaimed in His name to all the nations" (Luke 24:47). This divine call was fulfilled by Peter (Acts 2:14–40) and subsequently extended to Paul (Gal. 1:15–16), Timothy (1 Tim. 4:14), and other gifted believers whom the ascended Christ would give to the church (Eph. 4:11–13).

Down through the centuries, the Lord has continued to build His church through His chosen instruments who are called to proclaim the Scripture (2 Tim. 2:2). This divine design remains the unchanging pattern until the end of the age.

Concerning this high calling, Martin Luther said, "If I could today become king or emperor, I would not give up my office as preacher."[4] What loftier appointment could be given than to be divinely summoned to proclaim the truth of Scripture? At the same time, what more humbling station could there be than to herald the gospel of Christ? Truly, if God calls you to be His servant, why stoop to be a king?

————

Has God called *you* to preach His word? Do you feel the pull of the Holy Spirit into this noble calling? How can you know if you have been divinely appointed for this mission?

The answers to these questions are of vital importance for the work of Christ. They are eminently strategic for the success of the church. And they are key for discerning God's will for your own life. Given the importance of preaching in the church, it is critical that you understand how to discern a call to the pulpit.

As you pursue God's will, it is necessary to recognize distinguishing marks that can help you decipher if you are being drawn into the ministry of proclaiming His word. If God is summoning you to preach, the following markers will be evident in your life.

A Burning Passion to Preach

First, you will feel an overwhelming burden to preach. A call to the ministry is made evident when you experience a burning desire for this work. A strong inner compulsion will drive you to give yourself to this sacred task. You will reach a tipping point in which you feel compelled to leave your present occupation to give yourself to preach. The secular vocation you once pursued so wholeheartedly now seems empty by comparison.

Your mind is now preoccupied with spiritual truths and eternal pursuits. You undeniably long to advance the work of God, no matter the sacrifice it may cost you. The work of preaching the word increasingly dominates your mind and drives your heart. This inner tug will not leave you alone.

This is precisely what Paul explains to Timothy: "It is a trustworthy statement: if any man aspires to the office of overseer, it is a fine work he desires to do" (1 Tim. 3:1). The two key words here are "aspire" and "desire." Both communicate a holy compulsion to serve in spiritual leadership. The word translated "aspire," *oregō*, is a rare Greek word that means to seek to accomplish a specific goal; it speaks of striving for something with a strong desire. This word describes the one who longs to step forward to serve God in the ministry. A building passion to preach the word burns within you.

The other critical word Paul uses in this passage is "desire." It is derived from the Greek word *epithymeō*, which means to have a strong desire to do or secure something. The meaning can be used either positively or negatively, depending upon its context. In this case, "desire" indicates a proper attraction for what is holy, namely a call to the ministry. This word describes a strong inner drive that motivates a person to enter the ministry. The desire is so overwhelming that you will make whatever sacrifice is necessary to fulfill this call.

Charles Spurgeon stressed that this strong desire to preach the word will be present in those called to preach. In his autobiography, he emphasized this necessity:

> If a man be truly called of God to the ministry, I will defy him to withhold himself from it. A man who has really within him the inspiration of the Holy Ghost calling him to preach, cannot help it—he must preach. As fire within the bones, so will that influence be until it blazes forth. Friends may check him, foes criticize him, despisers sneer at him, the man is indomitable; he must preach if he has the call of heaven.[5]

This all-consuming desire to proclaim the word is the leading indicator of a call to the ministry. Such a one would rather die than not be in gospel ministry; they feel that strongly about being involved in the work of God. Gospel work is not something you merely want to do but *must* do.

Martyn Lloyd-Jones himself experienced this overwhelming desire to preach the word. While in his twenties, Lloyd-Jones had already ascended to a prominent place in the British medical community as a brilliant physician. The future seemed to be in his hands for the taking. But God had other plans. The Lord began to stir his soul, and he became increasingly dissatisfied with his successful medical practice. Despite this elite position, Lloyd-Jones was restless and unfulfilled. As he treated many of the affluent in British society, it struck him that he was helping unconverted people become well so they could return to a life of sin.

> We spend most of our time rendering people fit to go back to their sin. I want to heal souls. If a man has a diseased body and his soul is all right, he is all right to the end; but a man with a healthy body and a distressed soul is all right for sixty years or so and then he has to face eternity in Hell.[6]

Though he worked closely alongside Lord Thomas Horder, the celebrated physician to His Majesty King George V, Lloyd-Jones realized he must become a physician not of the body but of the soul. He felt that he *had* to give his life to treat the deepest needs of men and women and invest himself in prescribing the only remedy for sin-plagued lives—the gospel of Jesus Christ.

This deep desire to care for the souls of others captured the heart of Lloyd-Jones. He felt burdened to preach the word of God.

I would say that the only man who is called to preach is the man who cannot do anything else, in the sense that he is not satisfied with anything else. This call to preach is so put upon him, and such pressure comes to bear upon him that he says, "I can do nothing else, I must preach."[7]

Do you feel this same longing for gospel ministry? Do you have a similar discontent with the world? If so, nothing else you can do will satisfy you. You can find no rest until you enter this labor of gospel proclamation.

A Marked Ability to Teach

Second, God's call to preach will be discerned by recognizing a Spirit-given ability to make His word clearly known. Paul states that those called must be "able to teach" (1 Tim. 3:2). Again, the apostle maintains, they must "be able both to exhort in sound doctrine and to refute those who contradict" (Titus 1:9). Those whom God sets apart to preach are gifted to teach the word and defend it when attacked. The Lord equips such persons with the supernatural ability to expound the Scripture plainly to others. This God-given capacity to teach through preaching is bestowed on those called into the ministry.

If you are called to preach, there will be a noticeable gifting in your life to rightly interpret the word with precision and clarity (2 Tim. 2:15). You will also be able to make the truth of Scripture clear to your listeners. If you are called to ministry, you will have an inner resolve to dig deep into the Scripture and discover its inexhaustible truths in order to teach them to others (Ezra 7:10).

This gift to teach will always be accompanied by a desire to study. These two—studying and teaching—always go hand in hand. As you teach in your preaching, you will be possessed with a deep desire to better know the word of God. Understanding biblical truth is necessary to help others lay hold of these realities. Though you may not have been a serious student in previous schooling, you should now have a new burst of energy to immerse yourself in studying the word.

Personally, I grew up in an academically driven home in which my father was a professor at a medical school. My younger brother followed in his footsteps to become a cardiologist and a professor of medicine. My mother had graduated first in her classes almost every year, and my sister was a well-respected schoolteacher. But my interest in studying was minimal at best. All I wanted to do was play sports, which was my chief focus through college. Needless to say, my lack of interest in school was a great frustration to my brilliant father.

This lackluster desire for learning continued after my graduation from college—until the day God called me to preach. Then I became gripped by a voracious desire to read and learn the Bible. This new desire was inexplicable, except for the fact that I was being summoned to preach. I was now consumed with a holy passion to study the word, read Bible commentaries, and learn theology. These two desires to study and teach are the heads and tails of the same coin. Wherever you find the one, the other will be present.

Do you have this strong desire to read and study the word? Can you teach with clarity the truth you are learning?

An Evident Growth in Godliness

Third, a call to preach will be evidenced by your ongoing conformity to Christlikeness. As you seek to discern God's leading, you should recognize His sanctifying work within you. A wholehearted pursuit of Christ will more and more dominate your life. You should witness deeper longings for personal holiness. Your prayer life should be expanding and your desire for godliness should be intensifying. No one discerns a call to preach while being spiritually lukewarm or entangled in worldly loves.

The depth of your spiritual growth is critical to discerning a call to preach. You will only detect this summons while you are spiritually blossoming. The condition of your walk with God is a determining factor in the ability to recognize that He is drawing you into a preaching ministry. But a lack of personal holiness is a certain indication that you are not ready to begin this process.

These crucial spiritual qualifications are listed in 1 Timothy 3:2–7. Paul writes that an overseer must be "above reproach," which means that no valid charge of habitual sin should be able to be legitimately brought against the one who desires to preach. Specifically, such a man must be "the husband of one wife," loving her with singular commitment, and must also be "temperate," meaning self-controlled, not swayed by the impulses of his flesh. Those who preach must also be "prudent," possessing discernment and wisdom in spiritual matters, and "respectable," demonstrating a recognizable spiritual maturity and dignity.

Further qualifications include being "hospitable," loving people, especially showing Christian love and concern for visitors and strangers, not being "addicted to wine" but under the control of sound judgment and uninfluenced by external substances, and not being "pugnacious," meaning not being a bully who is needlessly combative with others in order to intimidate and get his way. Preachers must also be "gentle" and "peaceable," acting graciously toward others, and "free from the love of money," not filled with greedy worldliness but freely generous.

Living an Exemplary Life

This godliness is important because preachers influence others not just through their sermons but through how they live. Jesus said, "A pupil is not above his teacher; but everyone, after he has been fully trained, will be like his teacher" (Luke 6:40). Every disciple must be being conformed into the image of Jesus Christ. The same will be true in the life of the preacher. You must model the message you proclaim.

Moreover, you must manage your own household well and exercise a spiritual influence upon your children, who, in turn, live in a manner that reflects your values. You should not be a "new convert" (1 Tim. 3:6) but show maturity in your spiritual life. And you must "have a good reputation with those outside the church" (v. 7), because you are visibly identified with the church in the community.

Your call to preach is confirmed by your close walk with God. This spiritual intimacy is evidenced by consciously living *coram deo*—before the face of God. You find yourself being drawn into closer fellowship with Him in order to rightly discern His leading in your life. While you are not seeking a mystical experience, nor are you hearing an audible voice, you nevertheless know the Holy Spirit is active in your heart, drawing you to love God more and more.

Discerning the Will of God

As you discern God's direction for your life, a desire for a closer walk with Him will be evident. When you study His word, different passages of Scripture will capture your heart in new ways. As you pray, you will long for the will of God to be done in your life and will plead with God to reveal the next part of His perfect plan for your life.

When you pray, you will be humbling yourself under the mighty hand of God. You are sold out to Christ with fresh abandon and consciously relinquish the direction of your life to Him, deliberately surrendering your future to God. In detecting the call of God upon your life, the lower you bow before Him, the higher He will lift you up and move you forward into His will. The more quiet and attentive you are in His presence, the louder His word will speak to you.

Shortly after his conversion, George Whitefield sought to grow in the grace and knowledge of Christ. He devoured the works of the Reformers and the Puritans, desiring to obtain a solid doctrinal foundation in the Scriptures. His search for knowledge led him to Gabriel Harris, a bookseller who would lend him books. Whitefield biographer Arnold Dallimore describes the unique practice Whitefield developed:

> [He prayed] over every line and word of both the English and the Greek till the passage, in its essential message, has veritably become part of his own soul. . . . When, in later chapters, we see him preaching forty and more hours per

week, with little or no time for preparation, we may well look back on these days in Gloucester and recognize that he was then laying up a store of Biblical knowledge on which he was able to draw amidst the haste and tumult of such a ministry.[8]

Whitefield devoted significant time to gaining a proper knowledge of Scripture, theology, and church history in order to become more godly and a more effective communicator of the gospel. He knew this was impossible without fervent prayer as he sought God's wisdom, grace, and discernment. It was in this spiritual mindset that Whitefield identified God's call upon his life to preach.

These same elements of godliness will be vital to your ministry. Before you can discern a call to preach, you must be living an exemplary life that is worthy of being emulated by others. This does not mean you need to be perfect to enter the ministry. If that were the requirement, no one would even come close to being qualified. But it does mean you must be growing in grace and seeking holiness. Your character, conduct, and conversations must reflect the message you will preach in the pulpit.

As you consider a call to the ministry, examine your life. Do you see these character qualities? Do you observe the grace of God shaping your Christian walk? This is a necessary step in detecting this calling from God.

A Strong Confirmation from Others

Fourth, you should receive confirmation from others that you are called to preach. This divine summons should be affirmed by those who observe your life and recognize your gifting. As they listen to you handle the word, they should offer affirmation of the clear evidence of your gifting to teach and preach.

In 1 Timothy 3:10, Paul says concerning deacons, "These men must also first be tested." This means a person must be given the opportunity to serve and be examined by others before being entrusted with a church office. The same principle applies for the one called into pulpit ministry. Before being confirmed, your preaching should first be tested. You should be observed and, if qualified, affirmed by wise people in your local church.

What others perceive in your attempts to minister the word is important. It may be the feedback of a close friend who hears you teach or preach. It might be the objective insight of an older saint. It could be the encouraging word of someone in a Sunday school class. Those in the church who hear you teach the word are often the most helpful aids in discerning whether you are called to preach. Sometimes spiritually mature people will recognize the hand of God upon your life before you sense it yourself. Their feedback will be invaluable to you in recognizing God's call.

A call to the ministry should also be acknowledged by the leadership of the church. The apostle Paul states that preachers must be "sent." This should be understood to mean a formal commissioning by a sending church. The apostle writes,

"Whoever will call on the name of the Lord will be saved."
How then will they call on Him in whom they have not believed? How will they believe in Him whom they have not heard? And how will they hear without a preacher? How will they preach unless they are sent? (Rom. 10:13–15)

In sending any preacher, the spiritual leaders of the church—its pastors and elders—must first examine the character qualifications and spiritual gifting of anyone being set apart to preach. They must affirm the validity of their call from God and test the integrity of both personal life and doctrine. Those who pass their appraisal should receive the laying on of their hands to validate what God is doing in their lives (1 Tim. 4:14), then be sent to proclaim the saving message of Jesus Christ.

If God is setting you apart to the work of preaching, the leaders of your local church should affirm this call upon your life. It is critical that you not be self-appointed to the ministry. Other people who are spiritually mature and ministry-minded should affirm that God is at work in your life in a special way. Only then may you have the assurance that you are being separated unto the work of the Lord.

One clear example of receiving the confirmation of others is the Scottish Reformer John Knox. After the martyrdom of his mentor, George Wishart, Knox was asked to teach a class of young men in St. Andrews Castle. He exposited the Gospel of John with such noticeable skill that he caught the attention of the older men present. When they urged him to vocationally preach, Knox adamantly refused. He believed he must not run where God had not called. A lay leader named John Rough soon thereafter preached a sermon, in the middle of which he publicly charged Knox to answer the call to preach. Terrified, Knox "burst forth in most abundant tears, and withdrew himself to his chamber."[9]

While locked in his room, Knox underwent much soul-searching. At last, he came to the realization he was being called by God. Now in agreement with those who had recognized his gifting, he stepped forward to affirm his call to preach. Here, the determining factor was the feedback of mature believers in the church. Knox offered himself to be the preacher of that congregation. In future years, he would become one of the most powerful preachers God ever gave to the church. But the recognition of his calling started with the confirmation of others.

As people in your life hear you teach or preach, do you receive their confirmation that you are uniquely gifted to proclaim the word? Do they recognize the hand of God upon your life for good?

Have you presented yourself to the leaders of your church for examination? Have they evaluated your qualifications for ministry? Have they affirmed you before the church?

A Spiritual Influence upon Lives

Fifth, you can know you are called to preach as you observe spiritual fruit in the lives of others from your ministry. The leading of God into the ministry is confirmed when you see people's lives being changed as you teach and preach the word. You will feel an overwhelming desire to see people experience a stronger faith in Jesus Christ. This prerequisite requires that you are spreading the gospel before you can detect a call to the ministry. When you cast the net in preaching the word, you will see souls being caught and transformed into the image of Christ. Your gospel labors will lead to new life in others.

This driving passion to see men and women converted to Jesus Christ was present in the life of the apostle Paul. He wrote, "I have made myself a slave to all, so that I may win more. To the Jews I became as a Jew, so that I might win Jews . . . to those who are without law, I became as without law . . . so that I might win those who are without law" (1 Cor. 9:19–21). Paul summarized, "I have become all things to all men, so that I may by all means save some" (v. 22). That is, he *must* see souls won to Christ.

This same goal to win people to faith in Jesus Christ will be present in all those called into ministry. Granted, only God can save a lost human soul. And only God can convict, call, and regenerate a spiritually dead heart. But He works through human means to accomplish His eternal purposes. This begins with Him calling individuals to preach the gospel. If someone is to discern a call to the ministry, there must be some evidence of the lost being brought to Christ.

Charles Spurgeon declared that he could not know for certain he had been called to preach until he saw his first convert. This confirmation came when he was seventeen years old, after he first began to preach. After a Sunday morning sermon, he heard an older woman had been brought to faith in Christ under his preaching. He visited her home later that afternoon, and upon hearing the testimony of this precious woman, he believed it was the seal of heaven upon his divine appointment to preach the word of God. He later recalled,

> How my heart leaped for joy when I heard tidings of my first convert! I could never be satisfied with a full congregation, and the kind expressions of friends: I longed to hear that hearts had been broken, that tears had been seen streaming from the eyes of penitents. How I did rejoice, as one that finds great spoil, one Sunday afternoon, when my good

deacon said to me, "God has set His seal on your ministry in this place, sir."[10]

Spurgeon testified that his aim to win souls to Jesus Christ dominated his ministry for the rest of his days. He asserted that he would rather be the means of saving one soul than the greatest orator on earth, would sooner see the poorest person saved than become the Archbishop of Canterbury, and would rather be the winner of souls than a king in theological debate.[11]

Martyn Lloyd-Jones maintained that God gives to those called to preach an evangelistic passion to reach lost people with the gospel. In such people, the Holy Spirit ignites a consuming desire for others' spiritual welfare. Lloyd-Jones wrote that the true call is accompanied by a heightened concern for the souls of others, a burden for their lost condition, and the desire to lead them to Christ for salvation.[12] This love for others includes the distinct realization that many people are perishing without Christ.

In his own life, Lloyd-Jones experienced this growing concern for others and their eternal destinies. He said,

> I used to be struck almost dumb sometimes in London at night when I stood watching the cars passing, taking people to the theaters and other places with all their talk and excitement, as I suddenly realized that what all this meant was that these people were looking for peace, peace for themselves.[13]

This spirited concern grew when he detected his call into the ministry, and this passion to win the lost continued to intensify throughout his life.

Everyone called into the ministry will be possessed with this same desire to bring people to faith in Jesus Christ. It must be more than a mere interest in learning the word of God. There must be a passion for the truth to reach lost souls. There must be some evidence of others being strengthened in their faith. Jesus said, "You will know them by their fruits" (Matt. 7:16, 20). This is true not only for the false prophets who produce corrupt fruit but also for the true preachers who witness godly fruit in their preaching.

As you evaluate your call to the ministry, do you see any evidence of someone being brought to personal faith in Jesus Christ? Have you heard the testimony of someone becoming a believer through your preaching or teaching? Do you see some measure of spiritual fruit in others that would allow you to move confidently toward this goal?

A Pressing Urgency in the Heart

Sixth, a call to preach usually creates a crisis in the heart. A call to the ministry is realized internally as you experience great internal turbulence. You are standing at a crossroads and must decide which way you will go. You are being pulled away from your former life and drawn into this new direction, but not without an intense struggle within you.

For Moses, this defining moment came when he stood at the burning bush and God called him to go speak to Pharaoh (Exod. 3:1–14). He trembled with a sense of his own personal inadequacy, asking, "Who am I, that I should go to Pharaoh?" (v. 11). For Isaiah, it was when he entered the temple in the year that King Uzziah died and encountered the holiness of God (Isa. 6:1–3). This was a disruptive encounter as Isaiah shook like a leaf in a storm. For Peter, James, John, and Andrew, this watershed moment was when Jesus called them to leave their fishing nets to follow Him (Matt. 4:18–22).

In each of these encounters, the call into ministry had these men leave their former life and pursue this new venture into the unknown. All were dramatic—and often traumatic— experiences in the lives of those called. No one yawned or felt apathetic when they were called. This pivotal moment was undeniably disturbing and soul-arresting. Even so, it will be disruptive for you, if you are being called. You will be shaken to the core of your being.

Describing this kind of a personal crossroads, Lloyd-Jones stated that when someone is called, there must be "an awareness of a kind of pressure being brought to bear upon one's spirit."[14] He identified this as "some disturbance in the realm of the spirit" in which "your mind is directed to the whole question of preaching."[15] Such an internal crisis becomes acutely alarming.

Lloyd-Jones suffered a soul-searching struggle over the call of God upon his life. He lost twenty pounds and endured many sleepless nights and finally came to a breaking point. His personal turmoil reached its zenith one evening when he and his wife, Bethan, along with another couple, attended the theater in London. When the play was over, the four exited the theater and Lloyd-Jones observed a Salvation Army band playing hymns on the street corner. This brave band proclaimed an open gospel witness to all who were walking by.

He was deeply struck by their unashamed witness for the Lord. As he observed this little ministry team proclaiming the message of salvation, their bold act became a pivotal moment in his life. He said to himself, "These are my people, these are my people I belong to, and I am going to belong to them."[16] It was at that moment that Lloyd-Jones resolved to shift directions and answered the call of God upon his life to preach.

For each person called, it may not be such a dramatic moment. However, the one summoned to the pulpit will often be confronted with an overwhelming sense of the pull of God. An enlarged awareness of the greatness of God will dominate their life, and an overwhelming humility will grip their soul, because the living God is making a claim upon them.

Can you point to such a pivotal moment in your search to discern the call of God upon your life? Have you felt such pressure in wrestling with this call?

An Open Door of Providence

Seventh, the one called to preach will be providentially ushered into the ministry through opening doors of circumstances. Where God leads, the path will be cleared so you can move forward to preach His word. There will be challenges, but God will sovereignly open the necessary doors and pave the way for you to answer His divine summons. Roadblocks will be removed, training will be made available, and resources will be supplied.

One example of God's providential dealings in a call to the ministry involved Paul's son in the faith, Timothy. God moved the apostle Paul into the life of this younger man as the chosen means to prepare him for ministry. The itinerant evangelist Paul traveled to Lystra, where he met Timothy and invited him to join his second missionary trip (Acts 16:1–3). This was not a chance encounter, but a divine appointment, one orchestrated by the invisible hand of our sovereign God. Behind the scenes, God was at work providing the future preacher with an older mentor who would train him for a ministry in preaching.

God worked similarly in the life of John Knox, as mentioned earlier, to prepare him for the ministry. God crossed his path with that of a powerful itinerant preacher, George Wishart. This traveling evangelist was shaped by deep Reformed convictions, which made such a profound impression upon Knox that he began to accompany Wishart in his preaching journeys throughout Scotland. The younger Knox became so close to Wishart that he became his personal bodyguard. His responsibility was to protect the older preacher with a broadsword against life-threatening dangers from the enemies of the gospel.

Though Wishart was soon martyred, Knox had witnessed firsthand the fearless preaching of the word. This was God's perfect plan to prepare him for the tempestuous lifetime of gospel ministry that lay before him.

What would an open door look like in your life? It may not be as dramatic as the situation in which Knox found himself, but it will be just as real and formative. It might be a pastor or a spiritual leader whom God has brought into your life to provide you with training and counsel for the ministry. This open door might be your acceptance into a reputable seminary for the biblical training you need to carry out effective ministry. Or it might be an unexpected financial gift or material provision that allows you to move forward into the will of God.

Whatever the door before you, it has been swung open by the invisible arm of God to advance you into your needed preparations to preach. Only God Himself can open these doors. He works through secondary means such as people and circumstances to provide these opportunities, but God is the primary agent who prepares the way that leads you to preach His word.

Are You Called?

Is God working in you to answer His call to proclaim His word? Is God pulling on your heart in a way that is becoming unmistakable? He may indeed be drawing you into vocational gospel ministry.

There is a story told about a captain steering his ship into a harbor. The entrance into the port was surrounded by a dangerous, rocky coastline. The captain knew he must line up three objects before he could proceed forward—the lighthouse, the church steeple, and the distant mountain peak. When all three lined up, the captain knew it was safe to sail ahead.

If you observe the indicators highlighted in this chapter take shape and "line up," you should move forward in answering God's call for your life. If this is where you find yourself, may God increase your faith to answer His call to preach. There could be no higher calling.

TWO

The Preacher's Mandate

PROCLAIMING THE WORD

The pulpit is the throne for the word of God.

Martin Luther[1]

The preachers who have made the greatest impact upon the church, as well as the world, have been those most committed to proclaiming the Scriptures. These heralds are deeply persuaded that the Bible is the inspired, inerrant, and infallible revelation of God. They are convinced that Scripture is authoritative and all-sufficient—an invincible weapon—and firmly believe that the kingdom of God best advances as His word is proclaimed.

If the evangelical church is to stand strong, it must be led by those who possess an unwavering commitment to Scripture and are persuaded that the spiritual health of the church depends upon the word being proclaimed with precision and power. They believe deeply that the work of God thrives the most where there is bold, biblical preaching in the pulpit. They know there can be no replacing this truth.

Tragically, though, many contemporary pulpits have become like dark clouds hovering over the congregation. They thunder loudly, but never produce the much-needed rain. In this spiritual drought, exposition is being replaced with entertainment. Theology has given way to theatrics. Doctrine has yielded to drama. Biblical sermons have been substituted with dry lectures and philosophical discourses. The pulpit has become a platform for glib talks and cultural commentaries. A state of emergency should be pronounced upon the modern-day pulpit.

If today's church is to be strengthened, decisive steps must be taken to recover authentic biblical preaching. A genuine revival requires a renewed commitment to expository preaching. We must recapture the life-changing power of the preached word and fill the pulpit once again with heart-searching expositions of Scripture. The church desperately needs leaders who will not play at preaching, but proclaim the truth, knowing eternal destinies are at stake.

The Signature Text

Any restoration of biblical preaching requires an examination of what is, arguably, the signature text on this important subject, 2 Timothy 4:1–5. This passage in particular stands above the rest as the sine qua non for the pulpit and serves as a chief cornerstone for our understanding of expository preaching.

Here, we find the last words the apostle Paul ever wrote. With this final message, the gospel torch is being passed from the aged apostle to his young son in the faith, Timothy. In a short time—perhaps only weeks, if not days—this veteran preacher will be taken from a dark cell in Mamertine Prison in Rome and, tradition tells us, will have his head severed on the main highway west of the city, the Ostian Way.

Paul writes:

> I solemnly charge you in the presence of God and of Christ Jesus, who is to judge the living and the dead, and by His appearing and His kingdom: preach the word; be ready in season and out of season; reprove, rebuke, exhort, with great patience and instruction. For the time will come when they will not endure sound doctrine; but wanting to have their ears tickled, they will accumulate for themselves teachers in accordance to their own desires, and will turn away their ears from the truth and will turn aside to myths. But you, be sober in all things, endure hardship, do the work of an evangelist, fulfill your ministry. (2 Tim. 4:1–5)

These words are preserved in Scripture for every preacher to strictly follow. In this hour, we desperately need to hear this apostolic charge. If you are called to preach, the gravity of this divine commission should weigh upon your fragile shoulders. May you sense the magnitude of these requirements upon your pulpit ministry. In these verses, God demands that you preach in the precise manner He prescribes. Jesus Christ is zealous for the proper proclamation of His word.

Some today claim we are free to preach in whatever way we desire. But nothing could be further from the truth—not if the Bible is to direct us. It is critical that this landmark text guide you in your pulpit ministry. It is necessary that you hear—and adhere to—these final words of the apostle Paul. Let us now look closely at this passage.

A Sober Charge to Hear

This admonition begins with the words, "I solemnly charge you in the presence of God and of Christ Jesus, who is to judge the living and the dead, and by His appearing and His kingdom" (v. 1). It is hard to imagine that any command could be more serious than this. It is unthinkable that anyone could read these words and step into a pulpit without being gripped with deep sobriety. You should contemplate this apostolic commission with fear and trembling.

The words, "I solemnly charge you," are an authoritative command to young Timothy. This verb, *diamartyromai*, means to make a solemn declaration about the truth of something. It signified an authoritative order issued by a commanding officer to a lower-ranking foot soldier that required the full obedience of the subordinate. A failure to do so would result in serious consequences. Paul's words are stronger, though, than any military order because they are issued as an apostolic command. Timothy had no option but to comply fully and immediately.

To affirm this charge, Paul appeals to the first two persons of the Trinity. He asserts, "in the presence of God and of Christ Jesus" (v. 1). These words are issued with the sovereign authority of God the Father and Jesus Christ. This charge comes *from* God the Father and Jesus Christ *by* the apostle *to* young Timothy. He must obey this charge, because he will one day appear before the Lord and give an account for his ministry.

Even so, this same commitment will be required of you, if you are called to preach. Many pressures will tempt you to compromise your pulpit ministry. Seductive influences will lure you to water down your message in order to be popular, and powerful forces outside the church will attempt to squeeze you into their mold. But here in 2 Timothy, it is the unrelenting pressure from people within the church against which Paul warns.

Dr. Albert Mohler, president of the Southern Baptist Theological Seminary, notes the present temptation in churches to sideline and subdue preaching in corporate worship:

> Many congregations are caught in a frantic quest for significance in worship. Churches produce surveys to measure expectations for the worship service. Would you like more music? What kind? How about drama? Is our preacher sufficiently creative in the service?[2]

The demands of many congregations and, sadly, even church leadership have led to these misguided diagnostic questions. Seeking to resist this dulling effect, Mohler argues, "Expository preaching . . . demands a very different set of questions: Will I *obey* the word of God? How must my thinking *be realigned* by Scripture? How must I *change* my behavior to be fully obedient to the word?"[3] These questions reveal an entirely different priority. They indicate that submission to the authority of God's word is paramount. On the last day, it will not be before people that you will stand. Instead, you will give an account to Jesus Christ Himself.

Paul intensifies the gravity of this charge by referring to Christ Jesus as the One "who is to judge the living and the dead, and by His appearing and His kingdom" (v. 1). Paul makes it clear that at the return of Christ, He will judge all people, the living and the dead. This includes every preacher.

Timothy will appear before the Lord and answer for his preaching. This examination will involve a review of the purity of his message and the motive with which he delivered it.

The Bible says, "Let not many of you become teachers, my brethren, knowing that as such we will incur a stricter judgment" (James 3:1). The words "a stricter judgment" should instill a deep sobriety in all who preach the word. Jesus maintained the same charge: "From everyone who has been given much, much will be required" (Luke 12:48). The responsibility to preach the truth brings a greater accountability to God. This is most true for everyone called to preach.

You should be greatly humbled by this reality. The one who preaches rises to the highest level of answering to God. Our current culture has a disinterest toward holy things, and the same apathy is reflected in many churches. In light of this, you cannot afford to be flippant or nonchalant in the pulpit. Neither can you be crassly edgy or profane as you stand to preach. Your congregation will never respect the Bible more than you do. If your listeners are to receive the truth attentively, your preaching demands your holy reverence.

A Supreme Charge to Keep

In 2 Timothy 4:2–5, Paul issues nine imperative verbs in rapid-fire succession. The first command, "preach the word," forms the overarching mandate for Timothy. "Preach," *kēryssō*, carries the idea of making an official announcement. It means to make something known by proclaiming it. It also carries the idea of declaring something openly before others with boldness. In this case, it was the word of God that Timothy must proclaim publicly to the world.

This word, *preach*, has a rich historical background. In New Testament times, the Roman emperor would issue an imperial decree in his palace. He would call for his heralds to come and entrust the decree to them. These official messengers would then carry it to the distant perimeters of the empire. They would journey to each outlying city, enter the marketplace, and gather people around. The citizens would put down their tools of trade, leave their businesses, and surround the official spokesperson, eager to hear the message.

The herald would raise his voice and issue a public proclamation of the imperial decree. This was not a time to stutter or stammer. Nor was it an occasion for any self-promotion or for lighthearted entertainment. To the contrary, the messenger would loudly and clearly issue the announcement exactly as it had been entrusted to him. He was not permitted to add any of his own opinions to the sovereign edict. Nor could he withhold any part of it.

The word for "preach" (*kēryx*) is discussed by Greek scholar Gustav Friedrich in the *Theological Dictionary of the New Testament*. Friedrich writes, "The herald does not express his own views. He is the spokesman for his master. . . . [H]e must keep strictly to the words and orders of his master."[4] It was the herald's sole duty to deliver the message precisely as it had been given to him. The anticipated response of the people was not to alter what he would announce. His faithfulness in proclaiming the message was to be his sole focus.

The message the apostle Paul charges Timothy to preach is "the word," the divinely inspired truth recorded in the Old Testament, the teaching of Jesus Christ as given to the apostles, and the books of the New Testament written at that time. Further, it will also involve the remaining books of the New Testament yet to be written. Timothy is charged by the apostle Paul to preach this word—and nothing else.

The definite article "the" indicates the exclusivity of this message. Timothy is not charged to preach *a* word, as though God's word is one of many messages from which he could choose to deliver. His message was not to be drawn from the pagan culture or secular society nor arise from the wisdom of worldly philosophers. Instead, he must expound *the* word that has come from God. The message to be preached is the one "inspired by God" (2 Tim. 3:16) and breathed out of the mouth of God Himself (Matt. 4:4).

Timothy—and every preacher—must preach *only* the written word of God. As theologian Walter Kaiser has said, "Every preacher needs to always have one finger in the Scripture, always pointing at the text he is preaching. Everything that he says must be coming from this text of Scripture."[5] That is, you must solely preach *the* word, because when the Bible speaks, God speaks.

A Specific Charge to Follow

Following this first imperative, "preach the word," comes eight imperative verbs in succession. Each subsequent command specifies the manner with which the word of God is to be preached. They direct Timothy in *how* the word is to be proclaimed. This is not a multiple-choice option in which he may select which ones he desires to keep and pass on the others. Rather, Timothy must obey all eight of these commandments. It matters to God *how* His word is preached.

Be Always Ready

First, Paul maintains that Timothy must "be ready in season and out of season" (2 Tim. 4:2). "Be ready" (*ephistēmi*) means to be ready to complete a task. It conveys the idea of fixing one's mind on something and being attentive to it. This word communicates a sense of readiness and urgency in preaching. A soldier must be always ready to go into battle at a moment's notice. A watchman must guard his post with vigilance. So must Timothy stand guard in his ministry. He must always be ready to preach the word.

There is no other season than being "in season and out of season." Timothy must be ready to preach when the truth is convenient or inconvenient, when it is welcomed or unwelcomed, when it is well-received or rejected. He must preach the word whether he is praised or persecuted.

Expose Every Sin

Second, the apostle Paul further tells Timothy that, as he expounds the word, he must "reprove" his listeners. To reprove (*elegmos*) indicates an expression of strong disapproval, reproach, or rebuke. The divine word is the plumb line by which every belief, thought, act, and word is measured. This bright searchlight exposes every sin committed in darkness. Expository preaching is intended to reveal the hideousness of sin for what it is: cosmic treason against divine sovereignty. As you preach Scripture, it must reveal what is unholy in the lives of your listeners.

For example, doctors who desire the health of their patients must diagnose whatever illness is in them if they seek to heal them. In like manner, preachers who would promote holiness in their listeners must unmask all sin in their lives. As they call for moral purity, they must bring out into the open every impurity. The word of God is like a sharp "two-edged sword" (Heb. 4:12). When unsheathed and rightly preached, it pierces to the depths of the soul, as far as the division of "soul and spirit." When the razor-sharp sword of Scripture is wielded, the heart is "open and laid bare" (v. 13), causing hidden sin to be exposed.

Call for Repentance

Third, Paul also requires that Timothy "rebuke" iniquity in his preaching. Rebuke (*epitimaō*) conveys the idea of expressing strong disapproval. It sounds an alarm that alerts listeners to the painful consequences of sin if they pursue wrong choices. A rebuke is a threatening caution that points out the inevitable repercussions for transgressions.

With a rebuke, you must issue calls for repentance and warn people to turn away from sin and to pursue a new life direction. John the Baptist did this when he cried out, "Repent, for the kingdom of heaven is at hand" (Matt. 3:2). You must plead with your listeners for a change of mind and heart that produces a change of will and life. Jesus preached, "Repent, for the kingdom of heaven is at hand" (4:17). Also, Jesus warned, "I tell you, no, but unless you repent, you will all likewise perish" (Luke 13:3).

Likewise, Peter issued this mandate: "Repent, and each of you be baptized in the name of Jesus Christ for the forgiveness of your sins" (Acts 2:38). Peter also announced, "Repent and return" (3:19). Paul proclaimed this same message, "solemnly testifying to both Jews and Greeks of repentance toward God and faith in our Lord Jesus Christ" (20:21). As you see, preaching must issue a strong message of repentance. Be faithful to declare the rebuke that calls for repentance.

Exhort the Listeners

Fourth, Paul writes that Timothy must "exhort" in his preaching. This word (*parakaleō*) means to call someone to come and stand alongside of you, to be at your side in order to receive comfort or counsel. It carries the idea of a call for action. After Timothy exposes sin and calls for repentance, he must exhort his listeners to pursue the right direction. He should plead with them to take necessary steps to pursue the will of God.

This is precisely how Timothy had observed the apostle Paul preach. Timothy accompanied Paul on his second missionary journey, when they came to Thessalonica. About their time with the Thessalonian church, Paul reminded them in his letter how he had exhorted them "as a father would his own children" to live rightly and "walk in a manner worthy of the God who calls you into His own kingdom and glory" (1 Thess. 2:11–12).

Paul later described his own preaching: "We proclaim Him, admonishing every man and teaching every man with all wisdom, so that we may present every man complete in Christ" (Col. 1:28). You must emulate this kind of preaching, which includes imploring your listeners to pursue the right course of action.

This exhortation, Paul also told Timothy, is to be done "with great patience." This word (*makrothymai*) means, literally, to bear up under provocation without complaint. It can also be translated *endurance* or *perseverance*. Timothy will face many challenges that will result from his direct preaching. Despite this adversity, he must endure the painful trials of ministry and remain patient with the people to whom he preaches, even when they are slow to obey and even resist it.

Paul's fledgling protégé has to be longsuffering in his preaching as he waits for people to respond to the truth. Undoubtedly, his listeners will need time to carefully consider the demands of the truths he expounds. There will be aspects of Timothy's preaching to which his congregation will be hesitant to adhere. Timothy must give them sufficient time to embrace what he is teaching and be "patient when wronged" (2 Tim. 2:24). Amid resistance to the truth, the Lord's bondservant needs to persevere with patience.

As Timothy reproves, rebukes, and exhorts, he must also do so with "instruction" (*didachē*). As he waits for his listeners to respond, he continues to teach sound doctrine. He must restate what he has taught and reinforce it when necessary. This instruction refers to biblical truth and the apostles' teaching. Timothy is to continually reaffirm what he has taught with additional teaching that brings greater clarity to the truth.

This heavy emphasis upon doctrinal teaching should mark your pulpit ministry. All preaching must include teaching that exposits the full counsel of God (Acts 20:27). Every preacher must be a theological expositor who teaches "the faith which was once for all handed down to the saints" (Jude 3). If there is no doctrinal instruction, there is no solid foundation for your preaching.

Be Sober-Minded

Fifth, the next command that Paul issues in preaching is "be sober in all things" (2 Tim. 4:5). But before he issues this imperative, Paul sets the context: "For the time will come when they will not endure sound doctrine" (v. 3). Throughout Timothy's ministry, Paul warns, there will be factions of apostasy in the church. He has already witnessed many professing believers depart from his teaching (Gal. 1:6). Those nominal church members became wearied with his didactic teaching. In due time, they showed their indifference to the truth. This will be the stiff opposition Timothy will face in the future.

Such carnal church members will want "to have their ears tickled" (2 Tim. 4:3). They will become intolerant of the doctrinal teaching Timothy brings and the imperatives to walk circumspectly. Rather, they will desire a feel-good message that massages their egos and tells them what they want to hear. They are too fleshly to receive sound instruction. He must not be naïve to this defiant response nor be surprised by their demands.

Paul warns these church members will "accumulate for themselves teachers in accordance to their own desires" (v. 3). They will sample various preachers until they find one who fits their carnal appetites and tells them what they want to hear. If Timothy does not accommodate them, they will cast him aside and find a new minister. Paul also warns him that the time is coming when people will not want to hear the truth he preaches that exposes their sin. In the face of this opposition, Timothy must resist catering to their sinful desires.

These self-deceived people, Paul writes, "will turn away their ears from the truth and will turn aside to myths" (v. 4).

The phrase "turn away" (*apostrophē*) was used to describe someone throwing a bone out of joint. As the word is preached, they will turn their ear away from the truth as if throwing their neck out of joint. Instead, they will be interested in "myths" (*method*) or religious superstitions. They will embrace the devil's lies that enhance their self-esteem while rejecting the truth.

What is Timothy to do when people reject his preaching? Should he tone down his message? To the contrary, the apostle charges him to "be sober in all things" (v. 5). To be sober (*nēphō*) means to be well-balanced and self-controlled. This term represents being free from all the intoxicating worldly influences to be brought to bear upon him. Timothy must not cave in to their demands to alter his message. He must not come under the spell of their desires. Nor be duped by their pandering. Instead, he is to keep his spiritual senses sharp.

Paul himself demonstrated this kind of sobriety when he refused to cave in to the pressures of becoming a people-pleaser: "For am I now seeking the favor of men, or of God? Or am I striving to please men? If I were still trying to please men, I would not be a bond-servant of Christ" (Gal. 1:10). No preacher can please both God and self-serving humanity. These two ambitions are mutually exclusive. He must choose one or the other. Paul was determined to please God.

Again, Paul writes,

> For our exhortation does not come from error or impurity or by way of deceit; but just as we have been approved by God to be entrusted with the gospel, so we speak, not as pleasing men, but God who examines our hearts. For we never came

with flattering speech, as you know, nor with a pretext for greed—God is witness. (1 Thess. 2:3–5)

Paul was not a cunning manipulator of people. Neither must Timothy—nor any man of God—become one.

Endure All Affliction

Sixth, Paul then commands Timothy that he must "endure hardship" (2 Tim. 4:5). In the original language, these two words are a single word (*kakopatheō*), which means to suffer misfortune and bear hardship patiently. Timothy must be willing to pay a high price for preaching the truth. In expositing Scripture, he will become a lightning rod in the electrical storm of escalating opposition. Amid this conflict, he must endure the discouragement that would cause him to want to quit preaching. He must persevere through tough times.

By remaining steadfast, Timothy will reveal himself to be a true man of God. It is easy to preach in good times, when everyone is applauding. But the authentic servant of the Lord will endure in preaching despite facing adversity (2 Cor. 11:23–30). For Timothy, preaching the word will mean persevering through rejection, ridicule, and persecution. It may even mean martyrdom, as it did for Paul (2 Tim. 4:6).

Evangelize the Lost

Seventh, Paul next charges Timothy, as he carries out his preaching duties, to "do the work of an evangelist" (v. 5). To "do" (*poieō*) in this context means to undertake a task. The "work" (*ergon*) pictures the demanding effort in proclaiming the Good News of Jesus Christ. Evangelistic preaching requires strenuous labor, wrestling with souls to win the lost to Christ. The work of an "evangelist" (*euangelistēs*) requires preaching the gospel to the unconverted, beginning with those in the church.

In gospel preaching, Timothy must start with evangelizing his own congregation. In his pastoral duties, he must call men and women to repentance and faith in the Lord Jesus Christ. This lies at the heart of his call to proclaim the word. Timothy must be always announcing the gospel of Jesus Christ and calling for drastic commitment to Him. Though the gospel is not in every biblical text, all verses can lead to the cross. This necessitates that Timothy must be always preaching the person and work of Jesus Christ and the terms required to follow Him.

Evangelistic preaching is what Jesus called His disciples to do. When Jesus summoned them, He said, "Follow Me, and I will make you fishers of men" (Matt. 4:19). They must not only cast the net of the gospel into the sea of a perishing humanity but must also draw it back in, pulling in those drowning with their strong gospel appeals. Peter gave this kind of soul-winning preaching on the day of Pentecost. The apostle proclaimed the death, resurrection, and enthronement of the Lord Jesus Christ (Acts 2:22–36) and then summoned the crowd to "repent" (v. 38). He "kept on exhorting them [to] be saved" (v. 40). The result was that three thousand souls were saved (v. 41).

In your preaching, labor hard in bringing the gospel to your listeners. You must toil to win them to Christ. There will always be tares sown among the wheat. There will always be empty professors among the true confessors. Admittedly, it is demanding work to herald the message of salvation to self-deceived people who are religious but lost. As you preach the word, exert every ounce of energy in seeking the conversion of souls.

Fulfill Your Ministry

Finally, Paul charges Timothy in his preaching to "fulfill your ministry" (2 Tim. 4:5). "Fulfill" (*plērophoreō*) conveys the basic idea of bringing a task to completion. It means to carry through an assignment to the end. Timothy must preach the whole truth God has entrusted to him. This requires the full disclosure of the word of God in his preaching.

This mandate requires that Timothy be outspoken. All that God says in His word, Timothy must speak openly. Paul writes, "But after we had already suffered and been mistreated in Philippi, as you know, we had the boldness in our God to speak to you the gospel of God amid much opposition" (1 Thess. 2:2). Such persecution did not cause Paul to soften his preaching. Timothy is to be just as bold, even when facing difficult opposition.

The same must be true for you. Do not shrink back from preaching the whole truth. Like Timothy, leave nothing unsaid. Every truth must be taught, every promise delivered, every hard saying declared, every sin exposed, and every controversy addressed. As long as God gives you breath, you must preach "the whole purpose of God" (Acts 20:27).

Follow the Directions

This strict charge is laid at the feet of Timothy. It is likewise extended to every preacher called by God and is the timeless

standard for all who preach. This apostolic charge rises above
the times in which it was first penned two thousand years
ago and continues to address every preacher today. This mandate transcends all continents and cultures. It applies to all
churches and pulpits in this present hour.

If you are called to preach, this is how you must carry out
this divinely entrusted assignment. This is what is required
of you. This is the mandate laid at your feet. Fulfill this
charge with supreme confidence that God will honor those
who honor His word.

In the sixteenth century, as the Reformation expanded,
the European continent was in an uproar. Kingdoms tot-
tered. Society shook. As the word of God was spreading,
some people came to Martin Luther and asked, "How do
you explain Europe being on fire? How do you explain the
Reformation?" Luther responded:

> I simply taught, preached, and wrote God's word; other-
> wise I did nothing. And while I slept . . . the word so greatly
> weakened the papacy that no prince or emperor ever inflicted
> such losses upon it. I did nothing. The word did it all.[6]

If there is to be another reformation in our day, the pulpit
must first be reformed. This kind of preaching commanded
by Paul must be recovered and restored to the contemporary
pulpit.

May you be one who is fully committed to proclaiming the
word in this day. May you preach with unyielding confidence
that Scripture possesses the power to do gospel work.

THREE

Behold Your God

EXALTING THE LORD

This is what preaching to the heart is intended to produce: inner prostration of the hearts of our listeners through a consciousness of the presence and the glory of God.

Sinclair Ferguson[1]

Those called to preach must be, as John Piper urges, committed to "expository exultation."[2] That is, your pulpit ministry must relentlessly magnify the supreme glory of God. Every sermon should be a coronation service in which you crown the majesty of God before the awestruck eyes of the congregation. As you stand to preach, unveil the splendor of God that is found in your text and declare, "Here is your God!" (Isa. 40:9).

Our greatest subject in the pulpit is always God. We must preach the glory of God first and foremost, before we declare anything else, and prioritize God for who He is. There is a popular maxim that says, "The main thing is to keep the main thing the main thing." That is true in our preaching— and the main thing is always God.

If our preaching is to be powerful, we must be preoccupied with the declaration of God. If lives are to be changed, we must proclaim His absolute holiness and the fullness of His grace and mercy. If souls are to be converted, if believers are to be matured, we must declare His abundant provision for all of life. Our preaching begins and ends with God.

Giving a Sense of God

In his famous lectures on preaching, Dr. Martyn Lloyd-Jones raised this probing question: "What is the chief end of preaching?"[3] His answer was, "It is to give men and women a sense of God and His presence."[4] He further clarified, "Preaching worthy of the name starts with God, with a declaration concerning His being and power and glory."[5] Lloyd-Jones certainly practiced this kind of God-exalting preaching and influenced a generation of preachers to do likewise.

How important is preaching a high view of God? A towering understanding of God leads to transcendent worship and holy living. But the preaching of a low view of God leads to trivial worship and base living. The spiritual life of any church is directly shaped by its knowledge of God. Our sermons should always elevate God and lead the people into "the knowledge of God and of Jesus our Lord" (2 Pet. 1:2). The highest goal of our preaching is that our hearers may "grow in the grace and knowledge of our Lord and Savior Jesus Christ" and, in turn, give Him glory (3:18).

The supreme aim of our pulpit ministry must be to give our listeners the lofty knowledge of God. We have been called to proclaim God, who "dwells in unapproachable light, whom no man has seen or can see" (1 Tim. 6:16). We need to unveil the radiant splendor of His majesty. We are called to preach this Most High God—lofty and exalted, perfect in power, incomprehensible in wisdom, and infinite in grace.

God is three in one—a Trinity. There is only one God (Deut. 6:4), who exists in three persons—God the Father, God the Son, and God the Holy Spirit (Matt. 28:19). All three persons are coequal and coeternal, each without beginning and without end. Because God is a Trinity, our preaching must address all three persons—Father, Son, and Spirit.

In this chapter, we need to discuss the trinitarian nature of preaching. We proclaim the glory of God the Father. We declare the cross of God the Son. And we do so in the power of God the Spirit.

Preach the Glory of the Father

In the pulpit, we must begin by declaring the glory of God the Father. This is how the Bible starts: "In the beginning God created the heavens and the earth" (Gen. 1:1). Everything in the universe finds its origin with God. So must our preaching begin with Him. Until we declare God, nothing else can be rightly understood. Apart from the knowledge of God, nothing else in life makes sense. We cannot understand ourselves, nor the world around us, until we behold God.

Not until we know who God is can the great questions of life be answered: Who am I? Why am I here? What is my purpose? Where do I find meaning? How can I know happiness? How can I be right with God? What is death? What lies on the other side of the grave? What are heaven and hell?

God-Saturated Preaching

This is why all our preaching must be saturated with the awesomeness of God. The Bible says, "Say among the nations, 'The LORD reigns'" (Ps. 96:10). Our message must pronounce His sovereign rule over the affairs of human history. We must declare that God exists and reigns over all creation. He towers over the nations. He rules over every human life and eternal destiny. "The LORD reigns" must be heard from every pulpit.

Throughout the Old Testament, the preaching of the prophets announced the perfect character of God. Moses declared God's holiness (Exod. 15:11; Lev. 11:44–45; 19:2). Isaiah did the same (Isa. 6:1–8). Daniel proclaimed God's sovereignty (Dan. 7:13–14). David magnified His loving-kindness (Ps. 136). Nahum announced His wrath (Nah. 1:2–8). Joel trumpeted His vengeance (Joel 2:1–17). All the prophets of old heralded the attributes of God.

In the New Testament, Jesus and His apostles proclaimed the greatness of God. Jesus preached the holiness of God (Matt. 5:48). He declared the Father is perfect in love (John 3:16), perfect in knowledge (Matt. 6:4), and perfect in His care (10:29–30). Peter's sermon on the day of Pentecost was a pronouncement of the mighty acts of God in salvation (Acts

2:14–40). Stephen declared that "the God of glory appeared" throughout the history of Israel (7:2–50).

In our preaching, we must do the same. Everything must center in God and seek to establish His rule in the hearts of men and women. Noted colonial preacher Cotton Mather said, "The great design and intention of the office of a Christian preacher is to restore the throne and dominion of God in the souls of men."[6] The message of every preacher is to declare the kingship of God over every soul. Moreover, we must pronounce that His kingdom will be established in those who believe in His Son.

Showing God's Greatness

Early in his ministry, John Piper decided to preach a message on the greatness of God in which he would make no personal application. He would simply pull back the veil and preach the holiness of God. For his text, Piper chose Isaiah 6, which speaks of the awesome vision of the transcendent holiness of God, enthroned in heaven. He deliberately gave not one word of practical application, which normally would be in his expositions.

As Piper recounted the effect of this message, he estimated that he never preached a sermon so practical. Hurting families were comforted and perceived needs were met. All because they had encountered the blazing holiness of God. Could there be any subject more practical than preaching God? Could any topic be more relevant?

In like manner, our preaching must be theocentric. We cannot allow ourselves to elevate lesser subjects. There are subjects of secondary importance we will address from the pulpit because Scripture does. But these are only peripheral issues. We must stress what is of "first importance" (1 Cor. 15:3): the glory of God.

The template for all our preaching could well be Romans 11:36: "For from Him and through Him and to Him are all things. To Him be the glory forever. Amen." God is the source, the means, and the end of all things. In the pulpit, our compelling passion must always be *soli deo gloria*—for the glory of God alone. "Whoever speaks, is to do so as one who is speaking the utterances of God . . . so that in all things God may be glorified" (1 Pet. 4:11).

Preach the Gospel of the Son

As we preach the glory of God, we must declare that He has supremely revealed Himself through His Son, Jesus Christ. The Lord Jesus is the "image of the invisible God" (Col. 1:15). He is "the radiance of His glory and the exact representation of His nature" (Heb. 1:3). The Son of God has come to make the Father known to us. Jesus announced, "He who has seen Me has seen the Father" (John 14:9). The main objective of our preaching must be to make God known by preaching Christ.

Paul adopted this mindset, saying, "For we do not preach ourselves but Christ Jesus as Lord" (2 Cor. 4:5). The apostle was constantly pointing his listeners to Christ. Summarizing his own preaching, Paul states, "We proclaim Him" (Col. 1:28). This was his sharpened focus in preaching. The heart and soul of apostolic preaching was the Lord Jesus. This singular vision of the person and work of Jesus must mark our preaching too.

This golden thread of Jesus Christ is woven through the entire Bible. Jesus affirmed Himself as the predominant message in the whole of Scripture: "You search the Scriptures because you think that in them you have eternal life; it is these that testify about Me" (John 5:39). After His resurrection, Jesus presented Himself as the unifying theme of Scripture: "Beginning with Moses and with all the prophets, He explained to them the things concerning Himself in all the Scriptures" (Luke 24:27). Here is your chief role as a preacher. It is to present Jesus as the grand theme of all of Scripture.

The Only Focus

The apostle Paul's singular focus in preaching Christ was magnifying the cross. Paul states, "We preach Christ crucified" (1 Cor. 1:23). The center gravity of his preaching was the saving death of Jesus Christ. No other emphasis in preaching must be allowed to rival or replace this primary truth. To preach "Christ crucified" meant that he must declare *who* Jesus Christ is—the Son of God and the Son of Man, truly God and truly man—and *what* He came to do: save people from their sins (Matt. 1:21). Only the God-man could accomplish this redeeming work of rescuing sinners.

Paul continues, "I determined to know nothing among you except Jesus Christ, and Him crucified" (1 Cor. 2:2). This Greek word "determined" (*krinō*) means to pass judgment upon or to engage in a judicial process. It carries the idea of rendering a courtroom verdict that cannot be changed. Paul is *this* resolved to proclaim Christ as irrevocable and permanent.

In his preaching, Paul does not teach the human wisdom of the Greek philosophers. He does not pontificate the empty mantra of worldly thinking or parrot the bankrupt tenets of secular humanism. Nor does he advocate comparative religion nor resort to positive thinking. Motivational pep talks are not an option for him. Paul is determined to preach nothing but Jesus Christ and Him crucified. He champions the atoning death of Christ, who saves all who call upon His name.

Paul boldly states that "the word of the cross is foolishness to those who are perishing, but to us who are being saved it is the power of God" (1:18). He believed that the cross divides all humanity into two groups: those perishing and those being saved. To those perishing, the cross of Christ is "foolish," both illogical and ridiculous. To the unconverted mind, his horrific death is sheer nonsense. But to those who believe, the cross is the power of God to save. The shed blood of Christ is the only means of delivering lost sinners from the wrath of God.

The Only Creed

In the sixteenth century, German Reformer Martin Luther understood that Jesus Christ must be his predominant subject in preaching. He cautioned, "Take Christ out of the Scriptures, and what will you find left in them?"[7] The answer to this question is *nothing*. Luther knew Christless preaching is powerless—and lifeless. He asserted, "The preachers have no other office than to preach the clear sun, Christ."[8] Luther was determined that every sermon must proclaim Christ.

Dedicated to this standard, the Wittenberg Reformer exclaimed, "A good preacher must be committed to this, that nothing is dearer to him than Christ."[9] No truth must be allowed to overshadow the proclamation of Christ crucified. Above all else, this central theme must be predominant in your preaching.

In the nineteenth century, this same Christ-centered focus was present in the preaching of Charles Haddon Spurgeon. Upon the opening of Metropolitan Tabernacle in London, England, Spurgeon ascended the pulpit to preach the inaugural sermon. The Prince of Preachers announced his text: "And every day, in the temple and from house to house, they kept right on teaching and preaching Jesus as the Christ" (Acts 5:42). In this first sermon, Spurgeon declared,

> I would propose that the subject of the ministry of this house, as long as this platform shall stand, and as long as this house shall be frequented by worshippers, shall be the person of Jesus Christ. . . . [I]f I am asked to say what is my creed, I think I must reply—'It is Jesus Christ.'. . . [T]he body of divinity to which I would pin and bind myself for ever, God helping me, is . . . Christ Jesus, who is the sum and substance of the gospel; who is in Himself all theology, the incarnation of every precious truth, the all-glorious personal embodiment of the way, the truth, and the life.[10]

In Spurgeon's preaching, Christ was *everything*—the only Savior of sinners, the Lord of heaven and earth.

Throughout his famed ministry, this Victorian pulpit giant magnified Christ. Spurgeon thrilled in extolling His glorious name. He would not be diverted from preaching Christ. He exclaimed,

The best sermons are the sermons which are fullest of Christ. A sermon without Christ, it is an awful, a horrible thing. It is an empty well; it is a cloud without rain; it is a tree twice dead, plucked up by the roots. It is an abominable thing to give men stones for bread and scorpions for eggs, yet they do so who preach not Jesus. A sermon without Christ! [Might] as well talk of a loaf of bread without any flour in it.[11]

This Christ-riveting focus by Spurgeon sets the standard for every preacher. Great preachers preach a great Christ. We must always be proclaiming Jesus Christ as Savior and Lord. Regardless of the culture in which we serve, or the expectations of our listeners, we relentlessly uphold the supremacy of His saving death.

Preach in the Power of the Spirit

To expound the greatness of Jesus Christ from the pulpit, we need the power of the Holy Spirit. This God-appointed task lies far beyond the abilities of any mere human. The expository preaching of Christ in a proper way requires the supernatural enablement of the indwelling Spirit. The best preachers are deeply aware of their dependency upon the Spirit.

Every preacher is a finite instrument in the hand of the omnipotent Lord. If our pulpit ministry is to succeed, we will succeed only by the power of the Spirit. We are weak and must rest in the all-sufficient energy of God's Spirit. If our preaching is to triumph, it will be "in power and in the Holy Spirit" (1 Thess. 1:5).

Paul recognized his own inadequacies when he asked, "Who is adequate for these things?" (2 Cor. 2:16). He understood that no one is capable to effectively preach the word by mere human ability. An exclusive reliance upon human talent and natural skill is utterly insufficient to do what is required in the pulpit. Paul's answer? "Our adequacy is from God" (3:5). The power and wisdom must come from God by His Spirit (v. 6).

Without the Holy Spirit, Jesus's disciples could accomplish nothing of any lasting eternal value (John 14:16–17). Jesus said, "Apart from Me you can do nothing" (15:5). Only by the Spirit would they be able to preach and "bear fruit [that] would remain" (v. 16).

Before Jesus ascended to heaven, He charged His disciples to preach "repentance for forgiveness of sins" (Luke 24:47). To empower them, Jesus explained, "I am sending forth the promise of My Father upon you," which was that they would be "clothed with power from on high" (v. 49). This "power" would come from the Spirit, who would enable them to preach the gospel. His apostles would proclaim the message of salvation through supernatural might.

On the day of Pentecost, the apostle Peter was filled with the Spirit (Acts 2:4) and empowered to preach a sermon that won three thousand souls to Christ (vv. 14–41). The sheer force of his gospel proclamation pierced their resistant souls. This power did not come from Peter, but from the Holy Spirit. His recall of Scripture was immediate, and his messianic argument was irrefutable.

Lloyd-Jones explains this ministry of the Spirit in the preacher:

> It is the Holy Spirit falling upon the preacher in a special manner. It is an access of power. It is God giving power, and enabling, through the Spirit, . . . the preacher in order

that he may do this work in a manner that lifts it up beyond the efforts and endeavors of man to a position in which the preacher is being used by the Spirit and becomes the channel through whom the Spirit works.[12]

If there is no power from God, the preacher in the pulpit is merely going through the empty motions of lifeless rhetoric. If there is no divine assistance, it is not preaching but merely a recitation of notes, and all words will fall flat. But if the preacher is filled with the Spirit, God will unleash His power in the sermon.

What will the Holy Spirit do in you as you preach the word? Here are five ministries of the Holy Spirit to empower your preaching.

Penetrating Insight

First, the Holy Spirit will illuminate your understanding of the biblical text. You will be enabled to comprehend the truth you are preaching with sharper focus. Under the influence of the Spirit, the meaning of the passage will become clearer in your mind. The Holy Spirit is "the Spirit of truth . . . [who] will guide you into all the truth" (John 16:13). He will bring the teaching of Scripture more distinctly into view. You will be enabled to see with greater insight into the passage you are expounding.

The psalmist prayed, "Open my eyes, that I may behold wonderful things from Your law" (Ps. 119:18). This request is what you should pray too. If your preaching is to succeed, you must be divinely taught before you can adequately teach others (1 Cor. 2:12–13).

Deepened Convictions

Second, the Holy Spirit will embolden your convictions in the truth. As you stand in the pulpit and in the Spirit, you will believe Scripture even more resolutely. A deeper commitment to sound doctrine will be cemented within you, and your assurance in the truth of the Bible will be galvanized. You will hold to the tenets of the faith with an even stronger grasp. Though you may be naturally reticent in temperament, the Spirit makes you bold as a lion as you preach.

This Spirit-given boldness was in Stephen as he stood before the Sanhedrin. Because he was "full of the Spirit" (Acts 6:3), he was "full of grace and power" (v. 8). As he addressed unconverted religious leaders, he was gripped with deep conviction in the face of his own martyrdom. In that moment, he became tenacious with the message of Scripture (7:2–53) and was anchored by the Spirit to the truth even unto his own death.

When Paul came to Thessalonica, he possessed the same unwavering conviction through the Spirit. As mentioned earlier, Paul writes, "For our gospel did not come to you in word only, but also in power and in the Holy Spirit and with full conviction" (1 Thess. 1:5). His preaching came "in word" and with deep conviction and power. The Holy Spirit strengthened him with a firm belief that the message would change lives.

This same boldness must be given to you. As you preach, you may be made immovable in your convictions. Everything you believe to be true will become further solidified as you stand in the pulpit. By the Spirit's power, the cross will be even more powerful to save. Heaven will seem more desirable.

Hell will appear more dreadful. You will preach these truths out of the greater depths of your convictions.

Inflamed Passion

Third, the Holy Spirit ignites within you an inflamed passion for God. The work of the Spirit will set your soul on fire for Him. You will possess a burning heart for the gospel that only the Spirit can give you. The Spirit will excite zeal within you to preach with urgency. This intensity is enlarged in the pulpit. However, if there is no passion, there is no authentic preaching. R. C. Sproul agrees: "Dispassionate preaching is a lie."[13]

There was passionate fire in Jesus's preaching. When He cleansed the temple, the disciples remembered Psalm 69:9 and saw its fulfillment in Jesus: "Zeal for Your house will consume me" (John 2:17). "Zeal" (*zēlos*) means an excitement of mind and fervor of spirit. The psalmist wrote that this burning desire would "consume" (*katesthiō*) the Messiah. When Jesus came, He was burning with desire for the honor of God's name.

This holy passion in Jesus was also seen in His preaching. He proclaimed the gospel with blazing intensity: "Now on the last day, the great day of the feast, Jesus stood and cried out, saying, 'If anyone is thirsty, let him come to Me and drink'" (7:37). His crying out was not merely to be heard above the crowd. Rather, Jesus was pouring out His soul as He invited sinners to come to Him.

As you are filled with the Spirit (Eph. 5:18), this fervency will burn in you. This desire is not self-generated but is from God. The Holy Spirit is often represented as a fire, producing heated excitement for the gospel (Acts 2:3). But a bland, dispassionate presentation of the gospel lacks the Spirit's enlivening enthusiasm. However, when you are filled with the Spirit, He will ignite your preaching for the glory of God.

Increased Love

Fourth, the Spirit will cause you to love those to whom you preach. The Spirit will cause you to long for the salvation and sanctification of your listeners. You will remain "in labor until Christ is formed" within them (Gal. 4:19). A new depth of godly desire for their spiritual development will fill your soul and cause you to keep "speaking the truth in love" (Eph. 4:15) for their greater good.

In His preaching ministry, Jesus was filled with overwhelming love for people.

> Jesus was going through all the cities and villages, teaching in their synagogues and proclaiming the gospel of the kingdom. . . . Seeing the people, He felt compassion for them, because they were distressed and dispirited like sheep without a shepherd. (Matt. 9:35–36)

Under the influence of the Holy Spirit (Matt. 9:26), Jesus was filled with "compassion" (*splagchnizō*) as He preached. Literally, this means to feel deeply in the bowels, or in the pit of the stomach. As Jesus preached, He felt pity in the depth of His being for their desperate condition. He yearned for their salvation.

Under the Spirit's influence, you will feel compassion and will be given a greater love for people. You will be moved to preach God's truth to them for their greater good. The Spirit causes you to deny your own self-centered ambitions and fleshly thoughts. He enables you to put to death the unhealthy desires for personal flattery and instead have empathy for hurting people. He makes you burdened to bring to maturity in Christ those to whom you preach.

Sustained Endurance

Fifth, the Holy Spirit will sustain you as you preach in your most difficult hours. Amid opposition, you will be made to stand strong by the indwelling Spirit. Apart from this internal power, you would be easily defeated by increasing resistance through spiritual warfare. But "greater is He who is in you than he who is in the world" (1 John 4:4). The Holy Spirit in us is far greater than any opposition we will ever face in our preaching.

As the apostle Paul proclaimed Christ (Col. 1:28), he was confronted with much persecution and suffering (v. 24). Nonetheless, he pressed on with endurance. He writes, "I labor, striving according to His power, which mightily works within me" (v. 29). This internal power was given to him by the Holy Spirit. Where others might have been defeated and quit, Paul persevered with much resilience to fulfill the call to preach.

The Spirit empowers even the most ordinary people. John Knox, the great Scottish Reformer, said, "God gave His Holy Spirit to simple men in great abundance."[14] Surely, you and I qualify for this. This divine empowering is the only explanation for how any preacher has the ability to be mightily used by God. Endurance in preaching comes from the

Holy Spirit. The strength to persevere in preaching comes from God.

Power in the Pulpit

Charles Haddon Spurgeon understood this need for the Holy Spirit in his preaching. This renowned preacher was fully convinced that apart from the empowering of the Holy Spirit, his spoken words would have little impact upon his listeners. He knew that to enter the pulpit without the power of the Spirit would be to embark upon a mission that could not succeed.

In 1861, when Spurgeon moved his congregation into the Metropolitan Tabernacle, it was the largest Protestant house of worship in the world, holding over 6,500 worshipers. As the Sunday morning service began, Spurgeon stood on the lower platform, where he led the congregation in singing and prayer. When it came time to preach, Spurgeon climbed a series of fifteen steps to reach an elevated platform that would allow him to be clearly heard by the massive throng of people.

As Spurgeon ascended to the pulpit, the heavy weight of his responsibility rested squarely upon his broad shoulders. Realizing the far-reaching impact of this sermon, Spurgeon felt his dire need for the Holy Spirit as he ascended the pulpit. With each of the fifteen steps, he silently repeated to himself this confession of faith: "I believe in the Holy Spirit. I believe in the Holy Spirit. I believe in the Holy Spirit!"[15] Fifteen times he reinforced this personal need for the dynamic power of the Spirit. Spurgeon knew that without this God-given strength, no sermon could prevail.

If Spurgeon, arguably the most gifted preacher since the apostle Paul, was utterly dependent on the Holy Spirit as he stepped into the pulpit, how much more must every preacher—you and me—rely upon His divine enablement. Every expositor must be empowered to expound the Scripture. Otherwise, our labor will be in vain.

Be one who declares the unrivaled supremacy of God. Trumpet the cross of Jesus Christ. Rely upon the power of the Holy Spirit. As you do, God will be honored in your expositions.

FOUR

In the Study

EXPLORING THE TEXT

At the heart of every pastor's work is bookwork. Call it reading, meditation, reflection, cogitation, exegesis, a large and central part of our work is to wrestle God's meaning from a book.

John Piper[1]

Having discussed the call and mandate to preach, we now want to address how to prepare an expository sermon. It is important we understand the different stages required in studying a biblical text and crafting a sermon. We need an overview of this entire process, start to finish. This skill will be developed over time and refined with much practice.

Picture a car mechanic. To be skilled in this work, he or she must be able to take apart a car engine and put it back together, knowing how each individual part functions, how they inter-relate with each other, and the order in which to reassemble the parts. All this is necessary to be a skilled mechanic, especially with the safety of lives at stake.

In the same way, the expository preacher must know the essential parts of a biblical sermon. He must know the in-terrelationships between each aspect of the message, as well as the sequential order in putting together each piece of the sermon. An effective expositor will be well familiar with each stage of this process. This is vitally important because the spiritual lives and eternal destinies of listeners are at stake.

The process of preparing a biblical sermon includes both studying the Scripture passage and preparing the message that explains and applies it. In this chapter, we will review the initial stages of studying a biblical text to be preached. Then, in the following chapter, we will address creating a sermon manuscript, which I would strongly recommend that you do.

It is said that a long journey begins with taking the first step. So, let us start down this path that will take us from the study to the pulpit. Here are the first seven stages of devel-oping a sermon drawn from a passage of Scripture. We will examine the next stages in the following chapter.

The Orientation Stage

Before you open the Bible to prepare a sermon, it is impor-tant to have a general orientation to the Scripture itself. No one can rightly study the Bible without some basic, working understanding of its content. If God has called you to preach, you should pursue the proper training that best prepares you to exposit His word. Training in the Bible is absolutely necessary before you can study properly. If you would be effective in the pulpit, you must have, at a minimum, a general orientation in each of the following areas.

Original Languages

Any proper study of a passage requires some knowledge of the Greek or Hebrew text, the original languages in which the Bible was written. At the very least, it requires being able to use study tools to access the necessary information in the biblical languages. Examining the words of your text in the original languages is essential to correctly interpreting a passage of Scripture. You need to be able to operate in the original languages—parsing verbs, performing word studies, and analyzing grammar and syntax. This will probably require attending seminary or at least a Bible college. Or you will need to acquire the resources to study your passage. A growing familiarity with Greek and Hebrew will sharpen your textual analysis.

Sound Interpretation

To rightly handle the word, you also must be taught the laws of proper interpretation. These rules enable you to discover the God-intended meaning of a passage and learn how to discern what its author meant to communicate to its original audience in light of the rest of the Bible. This requires understanding the passage within its historical and cultural context. You cannot impose modern ways of thinking upon the ancient text and expect to understand its meaning. These laws will be discussed later in this chapter.

Biblical Exegesis

You also need to have an understanding of the grammar of the biblical text and know how the words and phrases of a passage relate to each other. This orientation will help you determine what the biblical author intended the original readers to understand. You must know syntax, which is the arrangement of words and phrases to create sentences. A passage is a coherent section in which each word is an important link in a chain that is connected to other words. Learn to see what contribution each word makes to form a sentence. Then you need to see how each sentence builds a paragraph of thought.

Systematic Theology

Any training in the Bible must include knowing the basics of systematic theology. This collects the many doctrines taught in Scripture and arranges them in categories. It addresses what the whole Bible teaches on a given doctrine or topic. Likewise, you need some knowledge in the continuity, discontinuity, and progression of doctrine from the Old Testament to the New Testament. There are also subcategories in biblical theology, such as by author, including Moses, David, Matthew, Mark, Luke, John, Peter, Paul, and others.

Bible Survey

Any training in the Bible should also include an overall introduction to and survey of the entire word, as well as the unfolding story line of the Scriptures from Genesis through Revelation. Being instructed in the major sections and literary genres of Scripture is essential. Further, a general knowledge of each book of the Bible is required, including how it contributes to the overall message of the word.

Church History

Proper training should also include instruction in the key periods and movements of church history. These great eras should be surveyed and analyzed in light of the doctrinal issues surrounding each period. Leading figures, strategic events, and pivotal controversies should be understood. A preacher who lives only inside a contemporary bubble will be disconnected from the larger picture of how those called to preach in the past have interpreted Scripture.

The Preparation Stage

In sitting down to craft an expository sermon, everything starts with preparing yourself, gathering your books, and securing a place to work with the necessary equipment. Here is where you must begin.

Sanctify Your Heart

Before you can prepare the sermon, first prepare your own heart. Your life must be right before your sermon can be right. As a result, you need to be wholeheartedly engaged in your pursuit of knowing God and walking in holiness. No preacher can take their listeners spiritually where he has not already gone, nor adequately teach what he has not learned and lived.

This prerequisite necessitates that you are born again and have the saving knowledge of Jesus Christ. You cannot preach the gospel with power until you have first received its message by faith. Moreover, you must be walking in close fellowship with the Lord. To be an effective preacher is to model the message you proclaim and be a living epistle of the passage you preach. This requires walking in humble submission under the lordship of Christ and pursuing personal godliness. Your sermon preparation begins with nurturing a right relationship with the Lord.

Secure the Study Tools

Moreover, you must have the necessary resources to properly study the passage to be preached. As a carpenter needs various tools, so you will need different tools to study your passage. Technical sources that undertake a careful exploration of the passage will help you dig into your verses and discover their meaning. These include reference Bibles, study Bibles, Greek and Hebrew texts, and other language tools. You will also need Bible commentaries, Bible introductions, Bible dictionaries, theological dictionaries, systematic theologies, and more.

If you are a graduate of a Bible college or seminary, you have already been exposed to sound exegetical and theological resources and may already possess these books. Or you may be self-taught, and if so, you have undoubtedly gathered a solid library of reliable resources to guide your study. Either way, such books are necessary for the faithful study of your passage.

Find a Quiet Place

To optimize your study time, you need to find a quiet place to carry out this work. This requires a secluded area free from distractions, such as an isolated room or private office. In that cloistered space, you will need a large flat surface such as a desk or countertop, as well as proper lighting overhead. Otherwise, your eyes will be strained, leading to diminished vision and headaches. You also need a comfortable but firm chair that will keep your back straight and allow you to study for great lengths of time, and office supplies, such as a computer, printer, paper, ink, stapler, staple remover, clock, and, if possible, a photocopier.

Set a Study Schedule

To maximize your time, you must know yourself and discern when you are most effective in your study. If the morning is your most productive time, give those hours to sermon preparation. Know how much time you require to study for your upcoming sermon and start the process with enough time to complete the task with excellence. Thought should also be given to what part of the week you are most productive. Those days should be dedicated to preparing your sermon. If you are preparing more than one sermon in a week, also consider which days you will devote to which message.

As a general rule, I would give my mornings to God, my afternoons to people, and my evenings to my family. I would go to bed early in order to wake up early. For me, my mind was the freshest in the mornings. So I would want to give as many of my early hours to God in prayer, Bible study, and sermon preparation as I could.

The Evaluation Stage

In choosing which passage you will preach, you must know the spiritual needs of your listeners. What is the most appropriate passage of Scripture that will produce the greatest spiritual good in their lives? The following considerations must be taken into account.

To Whom Will You Be Preaching?

Are you preaching to a church congregation? Or a college ministry? A Christian school? If so, how well have they been taught the word? Are they mostly committed believers in Jesus Christ? Or do you discern that a large number are unconverted? What are their spiritual needs? Your primary concern should be meeting the needs of your listeners. Before you exegete a passage, you need to exegete your listeners.

Where Will You Be Preaching?

Where will your sermon be preached? Will it be in a church worship service? If so, will it be Sunday morning, Sunday evening, or a midweek service? Will this sermon be given at a Bible conference or at a retreat setting? Will this message be for a Bible class? Each of these settings will have its own personality. Some will be more formal and structured, others less so. You will want to consider the setting in selecting your passage.

How Much Time Do You Have?

The amount of time you have to preach is always a consideration. Some Scripture passages require more time to explain than others. In choosing what to preach, you need to consider that some portions of the Bible require more time to study and prepare the sermon than others. This will also have an effect upon how many verses you choose to preach.

What Did You Previously Preach?

If you have been preaching to this group from the New Testament, it could be time for you to shift to the Old Testament, or vice versa. If you have been preaching an epistle, should you preach one of the four Gospels? Is it time for Hebrew poetry? If you have been preaching a long book, you may want to turn next to a short book.

What Input Have You Received?

You may want to ask others what they perceive would be most helpful for your listeners, such as seeking the input of church leaders and teachers in the congregation. You could ask trusted people, "What do you think would be best to study next?" If your church uses a ministry calendar, pay attention to those expositions already planned. This gathering of collective wisdom will give you a broader perspective concerning where the church is spiritually and what it needs. What would be most edifying for them?

What Are Others Teaching?

You will also want to consider what other teachers in the church are teaching. You should stay in regular communication with them regarding the subject matter of their classes.

If the largest Bible class in the church is studying a particular book in the Bible, you probably will not want to choose it to preach. Wisdom would dictate that there would be too much repetition to double up on the same book. Likewise, if the previous pastor recently preached through a book in the Bible, it would probably be unwise to preach the same book. Comparisons would be inevitable.

What Resources Are Available?

You should also determine if you have the necessary study resources to undertake this particular sermon or series of messages. Having the proper Bible commentaries will be a necessary consideration before you launch a new book study or doctrinal topic. Be sure you can secure these tools before starting the first sermon. This will prevent you from spending needless time going in the wrong direction. Otherwise, you may end up in the middle of the series only to discover that you were unaware of a major interpretive issue that you misunderstood.

What Is Burning in Your Heart?

Ultimately, you will want to preach what is burning in your own heart. You cannot preach someone else's passion. What you select must light a fire in your own bones for whatever you take into the pulpit. What part of Scripture is tugging at your own heart and will not let you go? What is calling out for your attention? What is stirring your soul? This should rise to the surface for your strongest consideration.

The Selection Stage

Choose a passage of Scripture from the different methods of exposition that are available to you. Will you preach verse by verse through books in the Bible? If so, you must decide what book you will preach. How many verses will you select? Will you preach through only a portion of a book? Or a biographical sketch of a biblical figure? Will you preach a doctrinal topic? Or will you preach representative verses of a book? Let us consider each of these approaches.

Sequential Exposition

The sequential approach is preaching consecutively, verse by verse, through an entire book in the Bible: you start in chapter 1, verse 1, and preach over many weeks, months, or possibly years until you reach the final verse of the book. To varying degrees, every verse is addressed and every truth is delivered. Several reasons can be put forward for making sequential exposition the predominant approach you take.

First, preaching verse by verse through books in the Bible addresses Scripture the way God gave it to us. God did not give us a topical index of various subjects. Neither did God give us individual verses. Instead, He gave us a library full of books. Sequential exposition preaches the Bible in the manner God wrote it.

Second, consecutive exposition best ensures that you address the full counsel of God. By preaching the entire book, no doctrine will be avoided. No hard saying will be skipped. No sin will fail to be confronted. Subjects you may have otherwise bypassed will now be taught.

Third, verse-by-verse exposition best models for your listeners how to study the Bible. This approach shows the importance of the content of your passage in the book. You will give more attention to the building argument of the book, and you will be more inclined to give the meaning of individual words.

Fourth, book exposition maximizes your time. As a preacher, you are never wasting time in search of what to preach next. You know you will always be preaching the next passage in the book. It relieves you of late-night panic regarding what to preach. In addition, what you studied in previous sermons carries forward to subsequent messages.

Fifth, preaching through books in the Bible promotes pastoral longevity. You have sixty-six books to exposit. You will never run out of passages to preach. Many pastors move on to other churches simply because they have run out of material and illustrations. But when you preach through books, you never lack new books to expound.

Sixth, sequential exposition ensures balance in your preaching. By this approach, you are most likely to be well-rounded in what you teach. There will be both doctrine and duty, as we see in Romans and Ephesians. Preaching through books prevents you from overemphasizing your favorite truths in the pulpit. This way, your hobby horses are generally left out of your preaching. You are always moving on to the next passage or the next subject.

Sectional Exposition

Some books are so long that it may be prohibitive for you to expound every verse. Yet those books are important and need to be preached. A better option may be to focus on a single section in the book, such as preaching verse by verse through one specific chapter or expositing a cluster of chapters. Especially if your congregation is not accustomed to book study in the pulpit, this may be a wiser choice to help acclimate them to expository preaching.

For example, preaching the entire Gospel of Matthew might be out of reach for you with your church. A better choice may be to preach only one portion, such as the Sermon on the Mount (Matthew 5–7). Or rather than preaching the entire book of 1 Corinthians, you could expound one chapter, such as chapter 13 on the virtues of love. Other examples would be to preach the Ten Commandments (Exodus 20), the upper room discourse (John 13–16), or the seven letters to the seven churches (Revelation 2–3).

Representative Exposition

For large books, a better approach might be to preach only a sampling of isolated verses. Here, you would select the high points of the book to preach. This might include the first chapter. You could also preach the verse or verses that contain the main theme of the book. Then, the most strategic verses or key chapters that best capture the central idea of the book could be preached.

If expounding the book of Isaiah, for example, you could exposit the individual sections containing explicit Messianic prophecies (chapters 6–7, 11, 40, 42, 49, 50, 52–53, 61, 63, and 66). Another example would be to apply this method to the largest book in the Bible, the Psalms. You could preach one psalm from each major category (lament, didactic, praise, and so forth). Or you could begin a series of sermons through multiple psalms within just one of these categories.

Biographical Exposition

You could also develop a study on a particular person in the Bible. Here, you would need to preach from a number of verses and present a biographical sketch of one biblical character or group of individuals. People love biographical studies because it is easy to relate to real people in the Bible. Also, it is easy for you to make practical application for the lives of your listeners. Further, the biblical character being studied becomes a vivid illustration in itself of godliness or failure.

For example, you could prepare a sermon or series of messages on someone like John the Baptist or other notable figures such as King David, Solomon, or Deborah. Likewise, you could preach a biographical series on a group of people. For example, you could bring individual messages on each of the twelve disciples. The same could be done for those with whom Paul interacted on his missionary journeys, such as Barnabas, Lydia, John, Mark, Silas, Timothy, Luke, Priscilla and Aquila, and others.

Topical Exposition

Contrary to what some may assume, topical exposition is a legitimate form of expositional preaching. With this approach, you select a worthy topic or doctrine and develop it from many different passages. This topic would usually be a truth taught in the Bible. To preach using this approach requires an adequate knowledge of systematic and biblical theology.

You might choose, for example, the doctrine of regeneration and trace it throughout the entire Bible. Starting in the Old Testament, you should carefully exegete and interpret each individual passage and show how it contributes to the overall teaching on this subject. Then you would proceed to the New Testament. Or you could preach multiple sermons through one portion of Scripture, such as John 3:1–11, and cite cross-references from the entire Bible. Likewise, you would show how the truth of the new birth relates to other doctrines in the Bible.

From these various categories, you should choose one approach to exposit Scripture for the unique opportunity at hand and determine which will best suit your purposes for this sermon. This, of course, presupposes much prayer on your part before making a decision.

The Observation Stage

After you make a decision regarding what approach to adopt and what passage to preach, you will need to begin an initial investigation of these verses. You should be like a detective walking onto a crime scene to look for clues in every detail. Every aspect of the biblical text is important. You will want to become keenly familiar with the passage.

Read the Passage

Read your selected passage repeatedly with an observant eye. A superficial reading of the passage will inevitably lead to superficial preaching, but careful investigation of the verses will lead to an in-depth analysis. You cannot interpret and expound what you do not see in your text. The observations you make are vitally important to the effectiveness of the sermon. So, begin by reading your passage multiple times with a keen eye.

Determine the Literary Unit

As you read the passage, identify its surrounding context and the larger literary unit in which it is found. This unit of thought will differ from one literary genre to the next. For narrative, the paragraph is the story itself. In a psalm, the literary unit is the stanza. With prophecy, the paragraph is the vision. In a discourse, it is the isolated truth in that part of the message. In an epistle, it is the particular subject addressed. You may choose to preach the entire literary unit or only a portion of it. In most cases, your sermon will stay within this one unit of thought.

Determine the Context

Next, determine the context of your passage. Start with the macro and move to the micro. Where in the Bible does this passage find itself? Where in the progressive revelation of the Scripture is it located? What has led to these verses? Where in the book is it found? What is the building argument of this book to this point? What verses immediately precede it? Context is critically important.

Ask the Diagnostic Questions

As you investigate your passage, you should answer key diagnostic questions. Who is the author? To whom is the passage written? When was it written? Where was the author located? What were the unique circumstances of the author and the recipients? How does this passage support the theme of the book? The answers to these questions will help you to interpret the book in its original historical context.

Identify the Important Words

As you read the passage, find the key words. Repeated words are usually crucial to finding the central thrust of the passage. Observe theological terms, contrasting words, modifying words, and figurative words. Look up any words with uncertain meanings.

Parse the Key Verbs

The movement of the passage often follows its verbs. Discover the main verb in the sentence. What is its tense, mood, and voice? What verbs are participles that support the main verb? What adverbs modify it? Simply put, the action of the passage is traced by following the verbs.

Analyze the Grammatical Structure

You must also give attention to the role each word plays in the grammar of the sentence. This involves noting the structure of sentences and what part each word plays. What is the subject, main verb, and object? Where are the prepositional phrases? What do they modify? What are the clauses? What nouns do the adjectives modify? Are they definite or indefinite articles? Do the words form a simple or compound sentence? What is the relationship between individual words in the sentence?

Trace the Transitional Flow

Look for transitions in the author's flow of thought. These markers are often signaled with a conjunction such as *but* or *however*, which signal a shift in the direction of the action. Or the conjunction may indicate continuity in the author's thinking. Words like *therefore*, for example, point back to what was previously said and pull the truth or idea forward to a conclusion.

Isolate the Central Idea

What is the central idea of the passage? The main point must be clear in your mind and should dominate your sermon. In this sense, every effective sermon should be a one-point sermon. You may have three or four homiletical points, but there should be only one central thrust. Everything in your message must be connected to this overriding theme.

Draft an Initial Outline

Next, begin to shape an outline for your passage. A good outline is like a skeleton, providing the basic structure upon which the muscle relies. So it is with a homiletical outline. A good outline should be simple, not complex, and move consecutively through the passage. Such an outline makes it easy for your listeners to follow your train of thought. You should have as few points as possible with as simple language as is possible. The shorter the wording of the homiletical point, the better.

Discover the Doctrine

Every passage of Scripture contains doctrinal truths, whether stated explicitly or implicitly. It is your task as an expositor to discover the theology in the text, incorporate it into your sermon, and teach it to your listeners. This necessitates that you know systematic theology and be able to identify the doctrine in your passage. Further, you must be able to present it in light of the teaching of the whole Bible.

The Interpretation Stage

As a preacher, you need to have solid interpretive skills and know how to conduct a scrupulous examination as you investigate the biblical passage you will expound. You must probe its verses to determine the author's intent and explore its many details. Your ability to dig into a passage of Scripture and discover its meaning is vital to preaching with accuracy and authority.

Having observed the details of your passage, you then interpret its meaning. What does the passage mean by what it says?

Assume the Literal Approach

You should assume a literal meaning of your passage unless it dictates otherwise. *Literal* means the normal or natural meaning of words. Be careful not to allegorize or spiritualize the words where that interpretation is not intended or warranted. Of course, the Bible uses figurative language and literary devices that must be taken into account. But by and large, the Bible is to be understood in a straightforward, literal manner. It is written in words that can be studied, parsed, analyzed, and taken at face value.

Specify the Literary Genre

The Bible includes more than only one form of writing. Depending upon the literary genre of your passage, it will be marked by certain distinctive features that will influence your interpretation. You should ask, Is it a narrative? If so, is this story descriptive or prescriptive? Is it law with promised rewards and punishments? Is it Hebrew poetry with parallelism and figures of speech? Is it a proverb with general observations of life? Is it prophecy with vivid images? Is it a parable with one main point? Is it an allegory with multiple points? Is it a discourse with a sermonic structure? Is it an epistle with tightly worded correspondence?

Probe the Linguistic Meaning

The Bible was written in Hebrew, Aramaic, and Greek, and examining the passage in its original language will yield a truer understanding of the text. As noted, key word studies, verb tenses, grammar, and syntax all require that you operate in the original languages. A Greek or Hebrew dictionary will reveal the true meaning of a word, and a lexicon will trace the word's use in various contexts.

If you are not yet familiar with the original biblical languages, a good interlinear translation of the Bible, with

Hebrew and Greek dictionaries, will assist you in understanding these linguistic nuances. Without access to the
original languages, you will be dependent on the exegesis
of other interpreters. To the extent that you can study your
text linguistically, your preaching will be more precise and
presented with greater confidence.

Conduct Word Studies

Utilize word studies in the passage's original language.
This will include either Hebrew for the Old Testament or
Greek for the New Testament. Identify the root word and
research its etymology. You may want to consider any extrabiblical uses of the term. Know what prefix may be added
to the root to make it a compound word. Trace the use of
this word by the same author in other passages and see how
it is used. Words may have a different meaning in different
contexts.

Be on the alert for the limitations and pitfalls of word
studies. A preoccupation with a word study to the neglect
of syntactical studies and cross-references can result in mis-
interpretations in your study. Taken by itself, a word study
may not delve deeply enough into the biblical text. Your
word study should always be combined with syntactical and
contextual observation. Nevertheless, operating at this level
in the original language is fundamental to sound exegesis.

Research the Historical Background

You must also study the historical background and trans-
port yourself back to the ancient world of the Bible to grasp

the meaning of the passage. Bible encyclopedias and dictionaries provide key information for your text. The culture of the ancient world was vastly different from today's society. Knowing the social practices and political milieu of that time is critical. So too is understanding its marital, agricultural, and financial practices, which is indispensable to unlocking the meaning of the passage.

Grasp the Geographical Setting

Understanding the geography of the ancient Near East can be necessary in unlocking the meaning of a passage. For example, if you are preaching on Jonah, when he is commanded by God to go to Nineveh but boards a ship to Tarshish, what does that mean? Where are these two places in relationship to each other? Are they in opposite directions? Or are you tracing the missionary journey of Paul? Where are the various cities he visited? A Bible atlas is an extremely helpful tool in identifying these geographical locations. Effective preachers will help their listeners learn where the Sea of Galilee is compared to Jerusalem and can help them see where Egypt is compared to the wilderness and the promised land.

Find the Book Theme

Every book in the Bible has one dominant theme unique to that book. No two books have the same central message. Every chapter and verse is connected with that central idea. You need to ask, What is the main theme of this book? How do these verses contribute to the understanding of this big idea? How do these verses link to the unfolding story of redemption?

Learn the Literary Devices

Also, take into account the literary devices used in your verses. These communicative features include differentiating between diagnostic and rhetorical questions. You must note the figures of speech by which the author arrests the reader's attention. Common devices include simile, metaphor, hyperbole, personification, anthropomorphism, and many more poetic terms. These words and phrases, while not meant to be literal, are designed to paint vivid pictures in people's minds that are impactful and memorable.

Connect the Cross-References

Always interpret Scripture with Scripture. No verse is to be understood independent of the rest of the Bible. Nor should you interpret the entire Bible in light of one verse. Instead, see each individual verse through the lens of the entire biblical canon. If your passage is unclear, search for another parallel passage that will make it clear. One part of the Bible never teaches anything contrary to another part. Therefore, turning to cross-references will help you ensure the accuracy of your interpretation.

Determine the Authorial Intent

Lastly, you should always seek the biblical author's intended meaning. The key question in interpretation is not what the passage means to you or to your listeners. Rather, the fundamental issue always is, What did the author of this Scripture intend to say? To fulfill this task, put yourself into the mindset of the biblical author. If we take the passage in a sense that is contrary to what the original writer intended, then we have departed from its true meaning.

The Consultation Stage

After doing your own study, you should consult reputable Bible resources, checking your findings against the work of trusted scholars. By comparing your work with noted theologians, you can best confirm your interpretations. You want to check your conclusions. Have you gone astray from reputable theologians with your findings? Never teach what no one else in church history has ever found in your passage. Any novel doctrine will surely be false teaching.

Check Study Bibles

A study Bible is a helpful resource to use in interpreting Scripture. Many such tools have become available in the last several years. The explanatory notes in the pages provide a quick reference to check your interpretation of a passage with noted teachers. These study notes are not intended to be a comprehensive commentary but do provide valuable insight into your passage and can help you determine whether you are on the right track in your interpretation.

Read Bible Commentaries

You will also want to consult several trusted Bible commentaries. You should check yourself with a variety of such resources. Look at commentaries written at a popular level, as well as those that are more technical, to get a full spectrum of insight into your text. These resources will help you discover what observations you may have missed in your study. However, take care that you do not use too many commentaries, which can lead to preaching that is overly academic and too dense for the average listener.

Reference Systematic Theologies

As you discover the doctrine taught in your passage, consult trusted systematic theologies. The idea is to check yourself to ensure you rightly understand this particular doctrinal truth in light of how it is taught in the rest of the Bible. No passage teaches the whole of the Bible's truth. A sound systematic theology will help guarantee that your understanding of this doctrine is correct.

Your Initial Exploration

These stages should complete your initial study of any selected passage. The care with which you explore your text will in large measure determine the precision and power of your preaching. A superficial handling of Scripture can only yield a shallow presentation of the truth. Focus on the depth of your study, and let God worry about the extended outreach of your pulpit ministry.

The importance of following these initial steps cannot be overstated. The effective exposition of any passage can rise no higher than your careful observations. Exegesis and interpretation are critical for accurate Bible study and sermon preparation, and these initial stages are the sure foundation upon which every effective sermon is built.

God will honor those who honor His word. He promises that His word will not return to Him void. God says,

> For as the rain and the snow come down from
>   heaven,
> And do not return there without watering the earth
> And making it bear and sprout,
> And furnishing seed to the sower and bread to the
>   eater;
> So will My word be which goes forth from My
>   mouth;
> It will not return to Me empty,
> Without accomplishing what I desire,
> And without succeeding in the matter for which
>   I sent it. (Isa. 55:10–11)

God will mightily use those who study carefully and preach His word accurately. Every preacher should dig into each passage and proclaim its unsearchable riches with increasing confidence.

After studying a passage, the natural next step is to compile your studies into a sermon manuscript or set of pulpit notes. Let us look at the following stages in the next chapter.

FIVE

Preparing Your Exposition

CRAFTING THE SERMON

Our sermons will be both easy to follow and easy to remember if they always have a clear structure.

Stuart Olyott[1]

There are no shortcuts to preparing an expository sermon. Any message that is true to the biblical text and delivered with life-changing effect requires careful thought and proper organization. Whether you have been preaching for only a short time or for a lifetime, and whether you preach in a rural community or in a booming metropolis, you should always be refining your skills to properly construct a sermon. You must be a lifelong learner in crafting Bible messages that impact your listeners.

A sermon has a unique literary and rhetorical form of its own. It is not a blog post. Neither is it a magazine article or a newspaper editorial. A sermon is not a term paper or an article for a theological journal. Nor is it an exegetical paper or a running commentary on the passage.

Think of a sermon like a house. There is an introduction, which is like the front porch. Its purpose is to provide curb appeal and interest the listener to enter the main body of the message. The introduction, like the front porch, should be proportionately smaller than the house and provide desirable easy access.

The main body of the sermon is like various rooms inside the house itself. Each room is like a heading in the message. No one wants to live in a house without interior walls. No one wants the toilet to be combined with the kitchen and the dining room. There needs to be separation. In like manner, each heading in the sermon needs to be distinct and provide its own living space.

Rooms also need windows that let light into them. Even so, cross-references and illustrations provide illumination to the sermon and allow the listener to better see what the passage teaches and requires. And as the rooms in the house are connected by hallways, so each heading in the sermon requires transitions that provide flow from one point to the next.

Finally, a house needs a back door, often built like a back porch. Like the front porch, it should be relatively small compared to the main house. This is how the conclusion of the sermon should be: relatively small but providing an easy exit out of the message.

Before Construction Begins

As we consider the process of writing a sermon, we need a blueprint to walk us through various stages of constructing one. The building of a sermon can be divided into multiple steps. Admittedly, there will be some variance in the different stages from one person to the next in how this is done, practically speaking. Nevertheless, whether you handwrite or type your message, and whether you construct a manuscript, use abbreviated notes, or speak without notes, it is first useful to survey the essential steps in crafting an exposition based upon a passage of Scripture.

Before we address writing the sermon, let us consider three questions.

Should You Write a Manuscript?

Should you write a sermon manuscript? My advice would be yes. Unless you are unusually gifted, I think the positives outweigh the negatives.

1. Writing a manuscript forces diligent study and careful preparation on the part of the preacher.
2. It causes you to organize your thoughts in a structured manner with linear thoughts and well-developed order.
3. It makes you think through your choice of words and vary your vocabulary.
4. It leads to giving prior thought to a practical application in your sermon rather than offering it extemporaneously.

5. It makes you think through a well-crafted introduction and conclusion.

Having said this, many gifted preachers do not bring a manuscript into the pulpit. John Calvin carried nothing into the pulpit except his Bible—only a Hebrew or Greek text. R. C. Sproul adopted the same practice of preaching without notes. However, for the rest of us, I strongly advise writing a manuscript or a similar equivalent. I would rather be overprepared than underprepared.

Should You Use a Manuscript?

Should you take your manuscript into the pulpit? Many preachers choose to do so, whether it is a printout, a handwritten copy, or displayed on a digital tablet. If you use it to preach, exercise caution to not boringly read your manuscript. Do not rely too heavily upon it. Few things are worse than for you to stare at your manuscript for the entire sermon rather than looking at the people. A face buried in a manuscript is a death blow to effective communication.

Should You Reduce Your Manuscript?

You may instead choose to reduce your manuscript to a few pages of notes or summarize your manuscript onto one page. Or you may have only a few key words before you. The advantage to this approach is that it will probably help you maintain better eye contact with your listeners. Also, it will help you be more spontaneous and natural with your expressions. What is important is that you have gone through the process of preparing a full manuscript. This forces you to organize what you will say and how you will say it.

If you are a young preacher, you may find that you will begin your ministry by using a full manuscript. Then, over time, the written notes you bring into the pulpit may become shorter. Eventually, toward your latter years of ministry, you may require only a few notes. Bottom line: use whatever method works for you.

———

Let us now survey the process of writing a sermon manuscript. Having studied your passage and gathered your observations and interpretations, as we noted in the previous chapter, you will now want to organize your findings into what will be a preaching manuscript or sermon notes. Your written manuscript should begin to fall into a logical development of thought. To accomplish that, you should implement the following steps in order.

The Explanation Stage

In this first step, you will begin to transfer your sermon preparation from a rough draft to a polished manuscript. For me, this does not begin with the introduction, but with writing the first homiletical heading. By and large, you do not yet know what you are introducing until you have written the main body of the sermon.

This stage of writing the sermon manuscript should start with setting the first main point of the outline into place. For most preachers, a sermon outline serves them well. It provides the needed structure for their message and helps prevent them from rambling off-topic. It also helps listeners follow along with the sermon.

As a general rule, you should reduce the outline into as few words as possible: less is more. Polish the headings of the sermon, putting them into their best form. More often than not, fewer headings are better than too many points. Also, using only a few words in each heading is better than using many words. You may choose to use a literary device such as alliteration, or maintain a similar phonetic sound at the beginning or ending of certain words in each heading, to aid the communication.

Once the first main heading is in place, your exegetical and interpretative content from the rough draft needs to be put into the manuscript. This step involves writing whatever is necessary to rightly explain the meaning of the verses covered under this first heading. This will involve word studies, verb parsing, grammatical observations, historical background, geographical setting, cross-references, contextual issues, doctrinal findings—whatever is necessary to properly explain the passage.

As this exegetical and theological content is inserted, it should be restated in a conversational fashion. Rather than sounding highly academic, wordy, and dense, you should write as if you could hear yourself preach this material. Write for the ear of the listener. A sermon should not sound like a term paper or encyclopedic article. The purpose here is to explain what is in the passage under this heading and what it means. Helpful quotes can also be added at this point.

This process of forming the outline and explaining the passage should be continued throughout writing the main body of the sermon: after the first heading is complete, the second heading should be added, followed by the necessary explanation of the verse or verses covered under it, then the third heading, and so forth.

Your outline may continue to be refined as the final form of the message progresses. In this sense, the manuscript is a living document, ever growing and always developing. Then you can weave together the various parts of your sermon manuscript or notes by adding smooth transitions to connect the material of one homiletical heading with the next. These transitions may contain helpful summary statements of what was communicated that pull together a unit of thought in your written document. Good transitions will hold the interest of your listeners. They are like well-constructed bridges that connect blocks of thought.

The Implication Stage

As you write the manuscript, lead your listeners to consider what is not directly stated in your passage but is clearly implied. This would include other related truths taught elsewhere in the Bible that are reasonably assumed from this text, or truths that are closely connected to the truth in your passage. An *implication* concerns what is inferred from your passage. It is a close consequence of your verse or verses. Put another way, it is a reasonable consequence drawn from your passage that needs to be stated.

The unstated implications of your passage enable you to expand the richness of its teaching. Based upon what is taught in your text, you should show its inseparable relationship to other interrelated truths taught elsewhere in Scripture. Its implications reach beyond what is explicitly stated in this verse, like threads woven together in a complex tapestry.

Showing the implications of your passage will enrich your sermon with theological depth and profundity, building upon the doctrine in your passage by teaching other inferred doctrines. As D. Martyn Lloyd-Jones reasons, "You cannot deal properly with repentance without dealing with the doctrine of man, the doctrine of the fall, the doctrine of sin and the wrath of God against sin."[2] This is to say, each doctrine in Scripture is inseparably joined to every other doctrine. It is the role of the preacher to show this unity with the whole doctrinal teaching of the Bible.

Demonstrating these implications requires showing the seamless unity of what the Bible teaches. To do so, you must have a profound grasp of systematic theology found throughout the Bible. Knowing the major categories of sound doctrine and how its various truths relate to each other enables you to preach not only what is explicit in your passage, but what is implicit and taught elsewhere in Scripture.

Teaching the implications of your text means you should also show what it reasonably assumes from the listener. Given what is taught in your passage, what does it imply concerning daily Christian life? Based upon your verse, what does it require, though not directly stated? For example, if you are preaching on the sovereignty of God, what are practical implications to be drawn from your passage? Sovereignty implies we should be bowed low in humility before Him. Further, we should worship the King upon His throne and obey His every command. Though this application is not explicitly stated in your passage, such required action is rightly implied.

The Application Stage

If observation deals with what the text says and interpretation with what the text means, application is focused on what the passage states that it requires. Application is making biblical truth so pertinent to your listeners that they understand how it should affect their lives. Your sermon preparation is never complete until the text is applied to the individual lives of your hearers. You should always ask, What is directly stated in this text that requires something from my listeners?

The purpose of application is to show the practical relevance of the passage—to show what is required based upon what is taught in this text. Imperative commands in the Bible must be delivered in a manner that obligates each hearer to obey its demands. The application should be direct, pointed, and specific. To help think this through, you may want to picture a cross-section of five or six members of your congregation seated before you. What does this text have to say to each of them?

This requires being in touch with the people to whom you preach and knowing their needs. What struggles, temptations, and worldly influences do they face? Likewise, keeping abreast of current trends in books, newspapers, and internet media will help reveal the specific lures and conflicting tensions of the world in which they live. Writing the application will force you to be more precise. You do not want to ad-lib your application any more than you want to spontaneously create your interpretation of the passage.

With your application, first address the heart attitude behind the action. Authentic Christianity is a heart religion that, in turn, produces a change in actions. Show how your passage should transform our desires and motives. Solomon writes, "Watch over your heart with all diligence, for from it flow the springs of life" (Prov. 4:23). The greatest commandment states, "You shall love the Lord your God with all your heart, and with all your soul, and with all your mind" (Matt. 22:37).

The best example of this is the preaching of Jesus Christ, who repeatedly stressed that the heart must be right before God. Jesus said, "Blessed are the poor in spirit," "those who mourn," "those who hunger and thirst for righteousness," and "the pure in heart" (5:3–8). The Lord also said, "Everyone who looks at a woman with lust for her has already committed adultery with her in his heart" (v. 28), "For the mouth speaks out of that which fills the heart" (12:34), "This people honors Me with their lips, but their heart is far away from Me" (15:8), and "For out of the heart come evil thoughts" (v. 19).

Be sure to stress that any positive step forward to implement what the passage requires can only be done by the grace God provides. Christianity is not a self-help movement. Our sanctification is the result of the indwelling Holy Spirit, who supplies the wisdom and strength we need to live in conformity to Jesus Christ. As Paul writes, "By the grace of God I am what I am" (1 Cor. 15:10).

Finally, your application should be as close to the explanation of the passage as possible. Each major part of the sermon should reveal its relevancy for everyday life. You should choose to weave action points throughout the entirety of your sermon that indicate the practical life-change required by your passage of Scripture. If you regularly save all your application for the end of the sermon, your listeners may fail to make the connection from the doctrine of the passage to what it requires in daily life. Well-placed application keeps them engaged during the whole sermon.

The Illustration Stage

You will also want to add sermon illustrations to your manuscript; they can be like open windows that shed light upon the passage. A good illustration can create interest, capture the listeners' attention, and help explain the truth of the passage. It can also increase motivation and help make the message unforgettable. However, the truth taught in the biblical text is always of foremost importance, while the illustration is merely secondary.

Where will you find such illustrations? First, look to the Bible. This allows you to use Scripture to illustrate Scripture and allows you to teach more of the Bible as you preach the Bible. A biblical illustration carries greater authority because it is divinely inspired. There is a particular gravitas and impact to an illustration drawn from the word of God.

You can also draw on illustrations from church and world history. Historical illustrations carry a weightiness about them. They are interesting to the listeners and hold their attention. And they often are motivational, stirring the heart of the hearers. You will want to draw also from current world events, including the arenas of politics, medicine, sports, and music. An illustration drawn from the contemporary scene can show the relevance of what you are saying. Care must be given, though, not to endorse any sinful worldviews or lifestyles represented in the illustration.

Likewise, you can use personal experiences from your own life. These episodes can help you connect with your listeners and endear you to them as you illustrate the passage. However, be careful to not portray yourself as the hero of your own story. When using yourself, it is best to be self-deprecating, not self-promoting.

The Introduction Stage

Once the main body of the message has been written, you are ready to add the introduction. This opening is important because it draws in the attention of the listeners. Remember, the introduction is like the front porch of a house and should be smaller than the house itself. A porch that is too large will draw too much attention to itself. Rather, it should complement the beauty of the house, providing easy access into it. In the same way, the introduction should be large enough to draw listeners into the sermon but small enough to not distract from its content.

The introduction should capture interest. Failing to capture the listeners' attention at the beginning makes it difficult to draw them in for the main body of the message that follows. A strong beginning is mostly likely to lead into a strong sermon. This may be done through various means, such as relating a current event, citing a striking quote, or raising a probing question. It could relate a personal experience, pose a hypothetical situation, or address a life-related problem.

The introduction should also announce the main idea of the sermon and make the direction of the message clearly understood. This singular focus will be the dominant theme for the sermon. If you tell people where the sermon is headed, they will be more likely to focus their attention on what you will be preaching. If you were to sit down after giving the introduction, the interest of the congregation should be so piqued that they would insist you stand back up and deliver the rest of your sermon.

The introduction should also set the context for the passage to be preached. You may include establishing where these verses are in the Bible, explain what was in the previous verses, or show where this passage appears in the unfolding argument of the book. You can also set the historical context for the time in which it was written, address where the author was at the time of writing, state why it was written, or address the circumstances of its original recipients.

At the end of the introduction, you may want to provide the sermon outline. If the outline is worded simply, you could easily state your main headings and the verses each one covers. You may find people pulling out pen and paper to write down the outline. This announcement can serve to engage them in the message at its very beginning.

The Conclusion Stage

After you have written the main body of the sermon and the introduction, you will need to draft the conclusion. The conclusion serves as the final word of the message. It helps seal the truth to the listeners' lives and may call them to pursue a particular course of action. They may be motivated to follow the biblical path laid out by those verses. Every sermon should finish strong with a clear call to action.

An effective conclusion should contain an appeal to the whole person—mind, affections, and will. Concerning their minds, you may choose to summarize or restate what has been said. If the gospel has not yet been explicitly included in this sermon, you may want to teach the way of salvation in Jesus Christ. This may also include refuting false ways of finding acceptance with God. Either way, the mind must be addressed.

Concerning their affections, the conclusion may also be a place to ignite the emotions of the listeners. Jonathan Edwards called it "raising the affections."[3] You want people to feel the impact of the truth, not just know the truth. Emotions are an important part of our being. Consequently, we want our hearers to be motivated to live what we have preached. This may be prompted by a poignant illustration or an inspiring quote. Or you may send a warning that raises the fear of God. A strong sermon should challenge the will of the listeners. They must be called to take decisive steps in response to the truth preached.

Concerning their will, a gospel appeal may be included for nonbelievers to respond to the message of the cross and to repent and believe in Jesus Christ. Such a gospel invitation should be extended in the imperative mood. There will inevitably be people present who are not yet converted and need to be summoned to Christ. Conclude with a call to action that appeals to their will.

The last step in constructing your manuscript is creating a sermon title. Whether or not you include it in a worship guide or bulletin or put it on social media, you will want to title the message. It will help people access the sermon if it is listed on a web page and can help create interest in the sermon. It also plays a role in communicating the big idea of the message. As a general rule, do not be too trivial with the title. It will be hard for people to take seriously a sermon that has a shallow or silly sounding title.

The Inspection Stage

Your sermon manuscript is now complete. You have studied the passage and composed your pulpit notes. This written document is what you will follow when you step forward to preach. By this point, the crafting of your introduction, main body, and conclusion should be finished. You will now want to review your sermon notes to evaluate their overall quality. As you survey what you have prepared, take the following action steps.

First, review the quality. As you review your sermon manuscript, you should discern its overall quality. Will the introduction grab the attention and interest of the listeners? Is the preaching outline succinctly stated? Are theological definitions communicated in easily understood words? Do illustrations need to be added? Are the quotations pithy and short enough? Does the sermon have impact? Is there sufficient application? Is there a place for exhortation? What encouragement and comfort does it offer? Does the sermon end with strength?

Second, review the length. As you gain experience as a preacher, you will be able to anticipate how many pages of notes you will need for a sermon. This is never an exact science, but the number of your pages does give you a general idea of whether the length of your sermon is where it needs to be. You may need to adjust, either removing or adding pages. It is usually better to have slightly too many notes than not enough.

How extensive are your notes? Are they written in complete sentences or an abbreviated style? This will affect the flexibility you have in the pulpit to adjust according to your time allotment. As another general note, you will want to have about 70 percent of what you will say presented in your manuscript. This provides enough margin that you will be able to add to what you have prepared in the moment of the sermon itself.

Third, review the accuracy. Are your Scripture references correct? Are your quotations from theologians accurately stated? Are your definitions of theological terms precise? Are your historical facts correct? One factual mistake in these areas will cause some of your listeners to pay more attention to your error than to the truth you speak and may cause some of your listeners to be eager to correct your mistakes. A better review of your notes will prevent such a distraction.

Fourth, review the balance. A review of your notes should also include sizing up the amount of material per homiletical point. As best as possible, you will want the same approximate number of pages per sermon heading. There will obviously be exceptions to this. However, having disproportionately too many pages of notes under one main point may indicate that you need to divide one large heading into two smaller ones.

Fifth, review the clarity. A look at your notes should also include examining the visual clarity of what you have prepared. Are they easy to read? Is there enough white space on the page to make reading easy while standing in the pulpit? Do your notes need to be spaced out more? Is what you are saying clearly evident? Are your sentences simple enough to be understood? If most of your sentences are not relatively short but rather too complex, consider how they could be streamlined.

Finally, review the flow. As you read through your notes, is there a noticeable progression of thought from beginning to end? Does each sermon heading build upon the preceding one? Are transitions from one heading to the next easy to follow? Do they smoothly connect each point?

The Internalization Stage

Once you review your sermon manuscript, it must be etched into your mind and planted in your heart. What you have studied and written must be rooted and grounded within you. You need to become intimately connected with your sermon. Your entire being—mind, emotion, and will—must be saturated with its content. You must *know* your manuscript and be able to freely recount its content, *feel* the truth you will preach, and purpose to *live* the message before you can preach it to others.

As you review your notes, you may choose to mark them up. You may want to go through your manuscript with a pen, underlining key words so your eye will most easily see them in the pulpit. You may opt to draw circles and boxes around selected words or add arrows in the margin to flag your attention. You may then want to return to your notes a second time with a highlighter and mark what you want your eye to be certain to notice as you preach. Or you may do this by changing the font size or color of what you typed.

You will develop your own routine of interacting with your notes. As you gain preaching experience, your personalized approach will become what you most naturally do.

Whatever method you choose, your purpose is to seal the content into your mind.

You may also want to mark up your preaching Bible. Ultimately, you are not preaching your notes per se, but rather the Bible itself. Your notes are only a visual aid to assist you in preaching the word. Therefore, it will be important to make sure that your eyes are focused on your preaching Bible. An open Bible is primary; your notes are secondary. You may want to underline or draw circles around key words in your passage, draw diagonal lines that separate your homiletical headings, or even write key words in the margin of your Bible that represent each main point of your outline.

The Intercession Stage

Lastly, you should pray through your notes and intercede for those to whom you preach, both believers and unbelievers. Prayer and preaching go hand in hand (Acts 6:4). You must petition God on their behalf, that He will bless your preaching of the word for their spiritual good. And you should pray for yourself, that you will be empowered by God to deliver His word as you stand to preach.

As you pray through your sermon notes, offer each truth to God for His approval and blessing. Ask God to ignite your heart to preach this sermon and make your message a fire in your bones. You should confess all your known sin, repenting of wherever your life fails to meet the standard that your passage requires. Ask for grace to better live the truth you preach.

Pray for the spiritual growth of the believers to whom you will preach. Plead with God that His word will be profitable in their lives. Ask Him to till the soil of their hearts so the seed of the word will bear abundant fruit; as the word is preached, believers will understand and apply the truth, and the word will transform them into the image of Christ.

There will always be unbelievers present when you preach. Jesus only had twelve disciples, and one of them was Judas, an apostate. Consequently, you should also pray for the unconverted who hear your preaching. Speak to God about lost souls before you speak to lost souls about God. Bring to God those who are outside the kingdom of heaven. Only He can open spiritually blind eyes to see and deaf ears to hear the truth. Only He can open closed hearts to believe the truth. God delights to answer prayers to rescue those who are perishing. Pray and preach, and leave the results with God.

Finally, you should pray for yourself as the Lord's messenger. Ask God to fill you with the Holy Spirit. Pray that you will be directed to say what God would have you to say. Ask Him how He would have you to say it. Pray for the strength needed to preach despite your many limitations and weaknesses. Pray for an increased love for the people to whom you speak. Above all, pray that God will be glorified through your exposition of His word.

A Completed Process

When the writing of your sermon is done and the internalizing of your sermon manuscript is complete, you should rightly understand the passage and perceive how it should impact the lives of your listeners. When you have written what you will take into the pulpit with you, you are now ready to serve the Lord by preaching this passage to your congregation.

Following the stages outlined here will help ensure your faithfulness to the truth of God's word. In the next chapter, we will discuss the actual delivery of the sermon. Not every well-written sermon in the study is well-delivered in the pulpit. In the pages that follow, we will consider some elements to make the proclamation of your message most effective.

SIX

Stepping into the Pulpit

DELIVERING THE MESSAGE

Draw a circle around my pulpit, and you have hit the spot where I am nearest heaven. There the Lord has been more consciously near me than anywhere else.

Charles Haddon Spurgeon[1]

When you step into the pulpit, you are walking onto holy ground. As you assume this sacred assignment, you are undertaking the most important task ever entrusted to humankind. You are opening the infallible word of the living God and becoming a mouthpiece for His divine revelation. You are proclaiming divinely inspired truth that alone can save and sanctify, strengthen, and satisfy.

In the last chapter, we considered the necessary steps required to properly study a passage and create a sermon manuscript. But merely composing a manuscript and internalizing it are not enough. You must be able to deliver it with life-changing power. Your pulpit delivery is crucial to the overall success of the sermon. The substance of the message is most important. But the reason people listen to one preacher over another often pertains to how the message is presented. Your effectiveness in the pulpit is determined by not only what you say but how you say it.

After a chef cooks a meal, it still must be taken to the table and properly served. As long as the prepared food remains in the kitchen, it is not helpful to those needing to be fed. The food must be brought, piping hot, to the hungry people. So it is with the preacher and the sermon. No matter how good the message is in the study, it must be delivered with a warm fervency to the listeners.

Let us now consider some key factors that contribute to an effective sermon delivery. What are some of the distinctives of a successful sermon presentation?

Preach with Humility

If your sermon is to connect with your listeners, it requires your humility in the pulpit. No one wants to sit under a message in which the preacher is condescending. No one wants to be talked down to by a proud preacher. A compelling sermon requires your own submission to the authority of God. To deliver a powerful message, you must be under the lordship of Christ.

Every preacher should be self-effacing, clothed with humility, and not be self-elevating above the congregation. The Holy Spirit works through lowly vessels: "God is opposed to the proud, but gives grace to the humble" (1 Pet. 5:5).

Never strut into the pulpit like a prancing peacock. To be empowered by Christ, you must die to self daily (Luke 9:23).

Noted Puritan John Flavel writes, "A crucified style best suits the preachers of a crucified Christ."[2] That is to say, preachers who have died to self best proclaim a risen Savior. J. C. Ryle writes, "Humility is the highest grace that can adorn the Christian character."[3] The lowliest preacher best heralds the lofty Christ.

I once heard James Montgomery Boice speak about the teeter-totter effect in the pulpit. Picture children playing on a seesaw. When one end is up, the other end is down—and vice versa. He noted that both ends could never be up at the same time.[4] Boice then applied this visual image to preaching. If God is to be exalted from the pulpit, the preacher must assume a lowly posture in the pulpit. But when preachers exalt themselves, God is pulled down before the eyes of their listeners. If God is to be lifted up, preachers must be humble.

Let us face the fact that too many preachers are constantly promoting themselves, habitually talking about their own triumphs. Their congregations are left to live their spiritual lives vicariously through their pastor's personal experiences. Is it any mystery why such a message is so hindered and lacking in spiritual power? Pride is a deathblow to effective delivery, but humility leads to better reception with your listeners.

Preach with Authority

At the same time, deliver your sermon with a note of authority. Such a command in the pulpit rests not upon your own authority due to your office, title, or age. Instead, your only authority in preaching resides in the authority of Scripture itself. It should be the word of God that you are bringing, not your own thoughts or opinions. Your most powerful sermons are the ones most filled with the repeated refrain, "the Bible says." To preach with commanding authority, an effective expositor must relentlessly speak and quote the word of God.

Those who heard Jesus speak recognized the authority with which He preached. When He expounded the law of God (Matt. 5:21–48), they observed, "He was teaching them as one having authority" (7:29). This means that as Jesus preached, He was not quoting other rabbis or their tradition to establish His teaching. To the contrary, He interpreted and applied the law of God as it was originally intended to be understood and lived when first issued by Moses.

The apostle Paul spoke with this same authority. He grounded his own words in the sovereign word of God: "This we say to you by the word of the Lord" (1 Thess. 4:15). In like manner, Paul instructed Titus, "These things speak and exhort and reprove with all authority. Let no one disregard you" (Titus 2:15). Speaking with the divine authority of Scripture is a fundamental prerequisite for every preacher. Real preaching comes with the force of the authority of God, who binds the conscience and commands the will of the listener.

Theologian J. I. Packer agrees: "Preaching that does not display divine authority, both in its content and in its manner, is not the substance but only the shadow of the real thing."[5] Consequently, as you preach the Bible, you must be deeply convinced that what you proclaim is true. Believe that those who hear you should be compelled to act upon the truth. You are not offering suggestions nor laying out options. Rather, when you preach the Bible, you are commanding your listeners with the authority of God Himself.

Preach with Clarity

Another mark of an effective delivery is clarity. You should be easily understood when you preach. Your presentation should be linear not circular, structured not scattered. The result is a clear and coherent sermon. As Philip Ryken writes, "Expository preaching means making God's word plain."[6] It matters not how precise and profound your sermon is if you are unclear to the listener. Clarity is never overrated.

The Reformers held to what was called the perspicuity of the Scripture. They believed that God revealed biblical truth in matters pertaining to salvation and Christian living in a lucid and coherent manner. They spoke of the plain way with which God spoke in His word. Therefore, they determined to preach in the same articulate manner with which the Bible is written. As William Perkins said, "The plainer the better."[7] Plain preaching is a priority for any effective sermon.

John MacArthur writes, "Good preaching begins with clarity of content. And clarity begins with a single, easy-to-recognize theme."[8] Your delivery can easily become cluttered with so much information that you obscure your main idea. What results is a message that resembles a data dump. Resist becoming so focused upon the micro that you lose sight of the macro. Do not become so intent on observing individual trees that you lose sight of the forest. Your listeners will become lost in the minutiae of your message.

Preach with Simplicity

Closely related to preaching with clarity is doing so with simplicity. This requires having a clearly identified central theme.

Your sermon must have one dominant thrust, not two, three, or five big ideas. Otherwise, your message will be disjointed and disconnected. A simple sermon outline is an important aid to simplicity in your delivery. If people cannot follow you in what you are saying, it matters little how correct you are.

In *Simplicity in Preaching*, J. C. Ryle notes,

> To attain simplicity in preaching is of the utmost importance to every minister who wishes to be useful to souls. Unless you are simple in your sermons you will never be understood, and unless you are understood you cannot do good to those who hear you.[9]

If you abandon simplicity, you might as well be speaking in a foreign language. James Usher once remarked, "To make hard things seem hard is within the reach of all, but to make hard things seem easy and intelligible is a height attained by very few speakers."[10] In other words, it requires an uncommon but necessary ability to make profound truth understandable to the average listener. Effective is the preacher who can explain profound truth in a simple way.

To accomplish simplicity, make sure your vocabulary is accessible. Limit your quoting of ancient languages such as Hebrew, Greek, and Latin. Keep your quotes from other authors short. Do not preach over the heads of your congregants. You are feeding sheep, not giraffes.

Preach with Continuity

To be effective, you also need to be linear in your thinking as you deliver the message. The progression of your thought needs to be straight-lined, not circular. A clearly identifiable sermon structure is critically important, and a discernible development of what you are presenting is also essential.

A well-structured sermon outline is helpful to maintain continuity—for both you and your listeners. Progressing from "one" to "two" to "three" is useful. Whether or not you actually say "one," "two," or "three" for each heading is secondary. What is important is a coherent sequence of thought that is logical and clear. Your train of thought needs to be recognizable to your hearers. Chasing rabbits is a sure way to lose your listeners.

Staying on track is necessary and staying on message is vital. A sermon is not to be delivered like an omelet, with all its contents jumbled together. Instead it should be served as if on a child's divided plate, with noticeable units of thought.

Repetition and transitions can help make continuity seamless. John MacArthur advises,

> The most helpful way of emphasizing your theme and outline is repetition. As you move from one point to the next, use brief transitional sentences to review the points you have already covered. Restate the central idea of the message as often as appropriate.[11]

These rhetorical aids help make the sermon appear to be one unified body of truth.

Preach with Fervency

Your heart must be excited and energized by the truth you preach. If the message is to burn its way into the hearts of your listeners, you must be fervent in your delivery. Passion is absolutely necessary to any pulpit presentation of truth. Without passion, a sermon becomes a dry-as-dust lecture. Your message will be contagious to your listeners when you are full of zeal, ignited by the truth.

Walter Kaiser writes,

> With the burning power of that truth on our heart and lips, every thought, emotion, and act of the will must be so captured by that truth that it springs forth with excitement, joy, sincerity, and reality as an evident token that God's Spirit is in that word.[12]

Truth preached with passion becomes contagious and spreads like wildfire. Kaiser adds,

> Away with all the mediocre, lifeless, boring, and lackluster orations offered as pitiful substitutes for the powerful word of the living Lord. If that word from God does not thrill the proclaimer and fill [him] . . . with an intense desire to glorify God and do His will, how shall we ever expect it to have any greater effect on our hearers?[13]

Dispassionate preaching reveals the preacher's lukewarm heart toward the truth. Preaching in monotone is not preaching at all. A dull delivery is preaching in name only, not in dynamic reality. Simply going through the empty motions of religious talk, with a lack of passion, falls short of the biblical standard of what true preaching is.

Genuine passion makes the sermon compelling. Like a fire draws the moth to the flame, fervency in the pulpit draws the hearts of your listeners to what you are saying. Zeal in the preacher conveys the importance of the subject matter. Passion is like the tip of a spear that gives the message a sharp point to penetrate hearts.

Preach with Sobriety

Further, be sober-minded as you preach. The weightiness of your message must be conveyed. If the fear of the Lord is the beginning of wisdom, then surely it is the beginning of all preaching. You must be a God-fearing person as you preach His word if you expect others to have the fear of God. The prophets called this "the burden of the word of the Lord" (Zech. 9:1). Deliver the sermon as though life and all eternity—heaven and hell—are hanging in the balance.

As the apostles preached, they "solemnly testified" (*diamartyromai*), meaning they seriously attested to the truth (Acts 2:40; 8:25; 10:42; 18:5; 20:21, 23, 24; 28:23). This kind of sobriety must mark your preaching with a gravitas that weighs heavy upon your soul. Only then will it weigh heavy upon the hearts of your listeners.

You should preach as Theodore Beza said of John Calvin: "His every word weighed a pound."[14] Puritan Richard Baxter said, "I preached as never sure to preach again. I preached as a dying man to dying men."[15] Such earnestness is one of the missing characteristics of the modern-day pulpit.

Preaching today has been described as a mild-mannered person standing before other mild-mannered people and warning them to be more mild-mannered. You must preach in the spirit of Spurgeon, who said, "We cannot play at preaching. We preach for eternity."[16] The pulpit is no place for flippancy or "silly talk" (Eph. 5:4). We must be sobered by the magnitude of the truth we declare.

You are an ambassador of the King, not His court jester, and you should come across as such. You are representing the Sovereign One, not yourself. God has called you to be an expositor, not an entertainer. You preach from a pulpit, not a stage. You must take the word of God seriously. When you do, the people will likely do the same.

Preach with Intensity

Your sermon delivery must demonstrate evident energy in your body and a voice marked by intensity. There must be an animation in you that rises above the pitch of dinner table conversation. True preaching requires a vibrant display of intensity. As you stand in the pulpit, your liveliness must be seen and felt by your listeners. There needs to be vigor in your delivery. The pulpit is no place for relaxed chatting.

John Stott sounds a much-needed alarm:

> To handle issues of eternal life and death as if we were discussing nothing more serious than the weather, and to do so in a listless and lackadaisical manner, is to be inexcusably frivolous. . . . For one thing is certain: if we ourselves grow sleepy over our message, our listeners can hardly be expected to stay awake.[17]

This is to say, God gives us a divine dynamic as we preach. Your fiery convictions will cause your delivery to impact the hearts of the congregation. "Nothing," Richard Baxter said, "is more indecent than a dead preacher speaking to dead sinners the living truth of the living God."[18] Your ardent spirit should inflame your listeners.

Think of intensity like holding a magnifying glass over a piece of paper under the hot sun of summer. The rays of the sun are narrowed down as they pass through the lens of the magnifying glass, and the heat becomes greatly intensified, causing the paper to smolder and smoke. Soon, flames start and spread to the whole piece of paper.

In like manner, intensity in your preaching comes from focusing on the glory of God. The more you gaze upon the perfection of His holiness, the more your heart bursts aflame for God. In turn, the more energy you will have in your preaching. Such a forcefulness in preaching is necessary for the message to be properly delivered.

Preach with Urgency

Your preaching must also come with a compelling sense of urgency. Impress upon your listeners that they must respond to the message *now*. Convey the immediacy of the moment. Your message requires action *today*, not tomorrow. The immediate need of the hour should cause your voice to resonate in your listeners as a sense of emergency comes through your words—a sounding alarm that arrests the attention of your hearers.

Lloyd-Jones argues that preaching with no urgency is not preaching at all:

If the preacher does not suggest this sense of urgency, that he is there between God and men, speaking between time and eternity, he has no business to be in a pulpit. There is no place for calm, cool, scientific detachment in these matters. That may possibly be all right in a philosopher, but it is unthinkable in a preacher.[19]

Do not merely ask your listeners to go home and think about your message. Like a lawyer addressing the jury, you must call for their verdict today. Press for a response. "Do not boast about tomorrow, for you do not know what a day may bring forth" (Prov. 27:1). "Behold, now is 'the acceptable time,' behold, now is 'the day of salvation'" (2 Cor. 6:2). In your preaching, this urgency for the listener to act today must come through your delivery.

Preach with Variety

Your preaching should also be marked by a range in your voice and vocabulary. As you preach, learn to alternate your volume. Neither a constant loud voice nor a continued low-toned murmur will be effective. The fluctuation of your voice is critically important to the effectiveness of your sermon delivery and often depends on the tone of your passage. Your volume also varies with the size of the room, the occasion, and the number of people you are addressing.

Throughout the sermon, your voice should rise and fall with both a prophetic edge and pastoral touch. There should be peaks and valleys in the tone of your delivery and a full spectrum in your voice, from loud to soft and back to loud again. This should be done only as it is natural and proper.

Your disposition also needs to be suitable for the setting. Raising your voice may underscore the importance of a truth. But some of the most impactful things you say may be when you lower your voice. There are times to accelerate and decelerate the pace with which you speak. At other times, dramatic pauses may be called for that will help draw in your listeners and sustain their interest in what you are saying.

You should also exercise a diversity in your vocabulary and manner of expression. The repeated use of the same words can be a distraction to your listeners, even annoying. Habitual use of the same word will soon reach a point of diminishing returns. In such cases, you will sound more like a broken record than a finely tuned messenger. Nuanced word choices keep the listener's ear attentive to what you are saying. Words on target clarify the message.

Some words are common terms that easily connect with the average person in the pew. Other words are rarer and enrich those who are better read. Yet other words are far less intellectually demanding and are more colloquial. These may connect with teenagers and even children. Such variance will help you connect with and serve each kind of person in your congregation. Rotate your manners of expression and say the same thing in different ways. This requires that you be constantly reading and enlarging your reservoir of words.

Preach with Accuracy

Finding the best word—the *right* word—is critically important. Learn to choose a specific word over a vague one. Choose a vivid word over a bland one. Use active verbs over passive ones as much as possible. Employ a relevant word over an archaic one.

Two of the most important resources I use in writing a sermon—other than my Bible, commentaries, and Greek and Hebrew language tools—are an English dictionary and thesaurus. If you are a preacher, words are the currency with which you deposit the truth in your listeners. Do whatever it takes to add more words to your vocabulary. Accuracy of word choice helps to communicate exactly what you intend to say and best represent the truth.

Writing a sermon manuscript also helps promote accuracy and precision in what you are saying. It causes you to think through what words best represent what you intend to say. Another factor that locks in accuracy is learning to speak with negative denial and positive assertion. In other words, you should say what something does not mean and then what it does mean. There can be no misunderstanding this way. Such a twofold presentation sharpens the exactness of your message.

Preach with Personality

An effective delivery also requires you to preach with your own unique personality. A mistake some preachers make is attempting to emulate other renowned preachers. This contradicts the reality that you have been uniquely created and gifted by God. You have a one-of-a-kind temperament and mannerisms. In your preaching, discover your own voice and develop it. You must speak as God has individually gifted you.

In his famous 1877 lectures on preaching delivered at Yale University, Phillips Brooks defined "real preaching" as "divine truth through personality."[20] Truth preached must be flavored with each person's unique personality. Be yourself.

Be natural. Preach with your own style. Each expositor must be careful not to try to be someone they are not. If you parrot another preacher, your delivery will be unnatural and awkward. At the end of the day, utilize the specific abilities God has entrusted to you.

Lloyd-Jones urges all preachers:

> Be natural; forget yourself; be so absorbed in what you are doing and in the realization of the presence of God, and in the glory and the greatness of the Truth that you are preaching . . . that you forget yourself completely. . . .
>
> Self is the greatest enemy of the preacher, more so than in the case of any other man in society. And the only way to deal with self is to be so taken up with, and so enraptured by, the glory of what you are doing, that you forget yourself altogether.[21]

Preach with Liberty

As you stand in the pulpit, you need an unhindered liberty to speak. Deliver your sermon with freedom of expression. A detailed preaching manuscript can be helpful in sermon preparation, but it can also be a hindrance to effective delivery. If you are overdependent on a full draft of your notes, you will likely be ineffectual in your delivery and will be constrained and confined. Being chained to a full manuscript can prevent lively spontaneity in the pulpit.

Heavy reliance on a full manuscript will also, to some extent, inhibit good eye contact with the congregation. In any successful sermon delivery, looking into the eyes of your audience is critically important. A minimalist manuscript allows for the Holy Spirit to more easily add to your thinking and your manner of expression in the pulpit. Spontaneity can be impactful and compelling. You will find that some of the most striking things you say in the sermon are unscripted.

If your head is buried in your notes for the whole message, it will become nearly impossible to engage with your hearers. You will be most effective when you rely less on your notes. Only then will you be free to interact with your listeners. As a general rule, you should only glance at your notes and gaze at the people. In other words, look at the people more than your pages. This requires that you possess a thorough knowledge of your notes and an awareness of what they contain and where each part is found.

If you are new to preaching, you probably have a smaller knowledge of Scripture and theology and will therefore need more pulpit notes than a more experienced preacher who should know more of the Bible. Over time, you will have a deeper well of truth from which you can draw, and as your knowledge of the Bible increases, the size of your manuscript decreases.

Preach with Sensitivity

In preaching, you should feel a genuine concern for your listeners. The success of your pulpit ministry largely rests in how you come across to them. They must sense your love for them as you expound Scripture. Show that you genuinely desire God's best for them. If you regularly tear them down with rebuke but rarely build them up with edification, you will alienate yourself from them. You must "[speak] the truth in love" (Eph. 4:15). Paul writes, "The goal of our instruction is love" (1 Tim. 1:5). Truth preached in love wins a hearing with the congregation.

The apostle Paul also writes, "If I speak with the tongues of men and of angels, but do not have love, I have become a noisy gong or a clanging cymbal" (1 Cor. 13:1). You may be right in your exegesis and accurate in your interpretation, but if you are devoid of love, you will be an obnoxious noise in the pulpit. He then adds, "If I have the gift of prophecy, and know all mysteries and all knowledge; and if I have all faith, so as to remove mountains, but do not have love, I am nothing" (v. 2). No matter how much you know, and regardless of how right you may be, speaking the truth without love is an exercise in futility.

Paul concludes, "And if I give all my possessions to feed the poor, and if I surrender my body to be burned, but do not have love, it profits me nothing" (v. 3). Regardless of how committed you are to the truth—even if you become a martyr in the flames—if you lack compassion, your preaching amounts to nothing.

Genuine love is demonstrated with a warm countenance in the pulpit. It is conveyed with a caring heart of concern and expressed with direct eye contact that is personal. It is communicated with warm and inviting gestures that welcome your hearers. It is expressed with tears of empathy and made known with a sincere voice of compassion.

Preach with Familiarity

As previously mentioned, eye contact is critically important if you are to be heard by your listeners. It makes them feel that you are actually speaking to them in a personal way, helping you establish rapport with the people to whom you speak. Again, as stated earlier, do not preach to your notes. Preach to the people before you. Do not look over their heads either, or they will soon do the same to you. If you want them to look you in the eyes, then do so with them.

If you stare largely at your notes, you could be called a "bubble preacher." That is, it is as if you are standing in a glass bubble—or a remote sound booth—separated from the congregation. Without eye contact, you are disconnected from the people to whom you are speaking. Be sure to look your listeners in the eye as much as you possibly can.

As you look at the people, do not stare at only one person. Depending upon how your listeners are seated, your eyes should scan the entire gathering, looking at those directly before you as well as those to your left and right, those closest to you as well as those farthest away. The full scope of where you look will draw in the whole congregation to what you are saying.

Preach with Visibility

As you speak, you not only communicate audibly, but also visually. You preach not only with your voice, but with your whole body. A sermon is not only heard, but seen. This is especially true of your hand movement. You should not stand in the pulpit with your hands in your pockets for the entire sermon. Nor should you have a prolonged death grip on both sides of the pulpit. How you use gestures in preaching is a critical factor in an effective delivery. You need to have a natural freedom with the use of your hands in a way that is congruent with your message.

Your gestures must be natural for them to be effective and hold attention. They cannot be rehearsed nor contrived. You will gesture best when you are not aware that you are moving your hands. They should be a natural extension of your body and voice, punctuating your emphatic statements. When your arms stretch out, you visibly express that you are inviting the listener into your close circle of concern.

You should use different kinds of gestures as well, not repeat the same motion, like a robot stuck in one gear. It does not take long for this to become a distraction to your listeners. I have been guilty of this in the past. There was a time when I preached in Ligonier Conferences, and R. C. Sproul would sit in the front row and mimic my gestures as I made them. Though it was somewhat distracting, it nevertheless got the much-needed message across to me: I need to move my hands more naturally.

Preach with Dignity

As we deliver the message, we must never forget that we are ambassadors for the King of Kings (2 Cor. 5:20; Eph. 6:20). We represent the high court of heaven and have been sent by the One who sits upon the throne. Along this line, I strongly urge you to dress in a manner that conveys the importance of who has commissioned you and the royal message you have to preach. A sloppy appearance or overly casual dress betrays the eternal importance of the message you proclaim.

Clothing differs from culture to culture, and one preaching venue differs from another as well. But as a general rule, present yourself as one who has a high calling on your life. Give a visual impression that you have a substantial message.

Again, you are an ambassador of the King of heaven. You should appear sharp, not sloppy, and well-groomed, not disheveled or disordered.

Further, as the preacher, you are the worship leader who is leading the congregation into the presence of the Lord of heaven and earth. Your dress should give some indication of this royal audience with the King of the universe upon His throne. You are a royal spokesperson of Jesus Christ, representing Him before humankind. Your attire should be consistent with the sacred trust that has been given to you by God. The Bible says, "Man looks at the outward appearance" (1 Sam. 16:7). People do, in fact, look at your exterior. That is an aspect of your delivery. God is a God of beauty and order. Your presence should reflect this.

The Dynamics of Delivery

While the substance of your message is always the first priority in any sermon, if you are well-studied in the word but cannot properly communicate the truth, it matters little. You must be able to relay the message to your listeners. Otherwise, your sermon will be like a bridge to nowhere. It will only span halfway across the chasm, failing to reach the other side where the congregation is seated. From the pulpit to the pew, the truth of Scripture must connect with those who need to hear what you say.

More could be said about effective sermon delivery, but these distinctives will serve to lay a solid foundation. As stated earlier, it is not only what we say that is important, but *how* we say it. By illustration, you can make the best scrambled eggs, but if you serve them cold, people will not want to eat them. So it is in preaching. You can prepare the best sermon, but if you deliver it coldly and dispassionately, your listeners will not want to receive it.

I tell my seminary students that each one of them essentially believes the same truths. The difference among them will be that some will know how to deliver the message more effectively than others. Some will have an engaging delivery, while others will be stiff and awkward. If we are to be effective, we must learn and master the art of preaching.

Before we leave this matter of an effective delivery, there is one more aspect to consider: making application in the sermon. Stay with me as we dive deeper into this crucial aspect of expository preaching.

SEVEN

Making It Personal

CONNECTING THE TRUTH

When a man preaches to me, I want him to make it a personal
matter, a personal matter, a personal matter!

Daniel Webster[1]

A sermon is not complete until it has been applied.
An exposition without application is like an airplane that never lands or a piece of mail that is
never delivered. Application connects the Scripture passage
to the lives of its hearers in order to make it practically relevant. It shows how the message relates to the individual
lives of the congregation and demonstrates what practical
demands the truth makes upon them. Where there is no application, there is no sermon—only a lecture.

When I was in seminary, I had a professor who said he was
going to listen to each one of us preach in our churches. He

warned us he would sit in the front row, and at some point in the sermon, he would hold up a large sign for us to read. There would be only two words on it: "So what?"

His point was profoundly simple yet simply profound. *So what* does this truth have to do with real life? Your preaching needs to have a "so what?" too. *So what* does your passage have to do with the daily lives of your listeners?

The goal of a sermon is not merely transferring information to the listener. That is only a means to a greater end. The ultimate aim of the message is the transformation of lives—and this requires application. This important part of the sermon challenges the life, convicts the conscience, and comforts the heart. Application spells out what the passage requires of the listener. This is indispensable to an effective sermon.

Connect Two Worlds

In his highly acclaimed book *Between Two Worlds*, John Stott states that an expository preacher must live in two worlds at the same time. As you stand in the pulpit, Stott explains, you belong to two completely different realms, separated by thousands of years. You belong to the ancient world of the Bible, and you belong to the contemporary world in which you and your listeners live.

From the pulpit, you must first travel back in time and immerse yourself in the world of the Bible, transporting your listeners back two thousand years to New Testament times—or further back, into the Old Testament era. Put them into a fishing boat on the Sea of Galilee with Jesus and His disciples or into a cave with David as he hides from Saul.

Have them climb Mount Moriah with Abraham or listen to Jesus deliver His Sermon on the Mount.

As you travel to the distant past, you must explain the meaning of the Hebrew and Greek words, describe the cultural distinctives, and show the geographical setting in which the biblical passage took place. You need to provide the authorial intent of the verses. In all this, answer the most fundamental question: What did the biblical author mean when writing to the original audience?

But there is another world to which your listeners belong: the immediate context of the contemporary world. As you preach, you must show your listeners the practical importance of the ancient Bible for their modern-day setting. Address all the challenges and alluring temptations they face and bring the wisdom of Scripture to bear upon their present-day issues.

What does this Scripture passage require from modern-day listeners? What is the practical relevance of this biblical text for their daily lives? The answers to these questions will force you to bring forward the ancient truth of the Scriptures into the current world.

With one hand, you reach back and lay hold of the early world of the Bible. With the other hand, you reach forward and lay hold of the listeners before you and the world in which they live. You must never let go of either realm as you relate the timeless message of your biblical text to the contemporary world in which your congregation lives. Bridge the gap and connect the ancient world of the Bible with the modern world.

As a preacher, you must show the practical relevance of Scripture to the pressing issues of this hour—how the Bible addresses the mounting pressures and complex maze of living in today's world. Anything less is not true preaching as measured by the standard established in Scripture.

Let us now address this subject of sermon application in the lives of our listeners. Because life is multifaceted, so must our application be made on many different levels. As we seek to make our preaching life-changing for our hearers, we must consider the many ways the word intersects with our personal lives.

Confront the Carnal

In the pulpit, one of your chief concerns is to expose sin in the lives of your listeners. Everyone to whom you preach has one major problem that is common to all humankind. That is the problem of sin—the sin of their mind, heart, mouth, and will. In order to care for people, you must expose sin. They must see that their greatest enemy lives within themselves.

This is how Jesus preached. In the Sermon on the Mount, arguably the greatest sermon ever given, the Lord began by saying, "Blessed are the poor in spirit" (Matt. 5:3). This is to say, the listeners must first recognize their own spiritual bankruptcy before they can receive redeeming grace. Jesus started at this point and exposed the depravity of the human hearts of His listeners.

When addressing the same multitude, Jesus said,

You have heard that the ancients were told, "You shall not commit murder" and "Whoever commits murder shall be liable to the court." But I say to you that everyone who is angry with his brother shall be guilty before the court; and whoever says to his brother, "You good-for-nothing," shall be guilty before the supreme court; and whoever says, "You fool," shall be guilty enough to go into the fiery hell. (vv. 21–22)

Jesus named this sin of anger in the heart for what it was: murder. His exposition of the word was designed to uncover the hidden pretense and hypocrisy of His listeners.

If you are to preach like Jesus, confronting personal sin must be a critical part of your application. Until sin is exposed and addressed, the truth remains at a superficial level. But as it unmasks sin and reveals it for what it is, your sermon is identifying a disease that needs to be surgically removed.

There is only one instrument designed to perform such spiritual surgery. That is Scripture, which is "sharper than any two-edged sword, and piercing as far as the division of soul and spirit . . . able to judge the thoughts and intentions of the heart" (Heb. 4:12). The word preached cuts to the bone and exposes the wickedness that lies beneath the surface. It lays bare the soul to bring about confession and repentance.

As you stand in the pulpit, open-heart surgery occurs when you unsheathe the sword of the Spirit—the word of God—and wield it in the strength He provides. As you proclaim the holiness of God, the listeners come under the knife that reveals what is unholy in their lives. As you expound the word, the light of Scripture exposes deeds hidden in darkness. As you preach the law of God, the presence of personal sin becomes painfully known.

Do you seek to expose sin in the lives of your listeners? Do you reveal the ugliness of sin? Do you depict it as loathsome in the sight of God?

Warn the Wayward

When Paul addressed the spiritual leaders of the church, he urged them to "admonish the unruly" (1 Thess. 5:14). Those who are "unruly" (*ataktōs*) are people who are, spiritually speaking, out of order. This was a military term describing a soldier who was acting with disorderly conduct—and needed to be warned to step back into line. In the church, those who are out of step with God's word need to be called to no longer be insubordinate to His teaching. Otherwise they will suffer painful consequences to wrong decisions.

From the pulpit, you must "admonish" (*noutheteō*), which means to put something into the mind. The idea is to warn people by putting into their thinking the consequences of wrong decisions. It cautions them about the effect of hurtful attitudes and improper behavior. In your preaching, there has to be this element of warning issued to your listeners if God's path is being neglected.

Jesus's preaching admonished His listeners of the serious consequences of failing to heed God's word. If they allowed anger to fester in their hearts, He forewarned them they would be "guilty enough to go into the fiery hell" (Matt. 5:22). If they cultivated lust in their heart, their "whole body [would] be thrown into hell" (v. 29). These stern warnings that Jesus issued when He preached reflect His caring heart that sought to deliver people from eternal danger.

The apostle Paul preached this same way. He stated, "I did not cease to admonish each one with tears" (Acts 20:31). He warned his listeners in Ephesus as he sought to divert them from the harmful consequences of choosing to go their own way, and he stated, "We proclaim Him, admonishing every man" (Col. 1:28). He cautioned people in danger of divine punishment. If they continued down the path of disobedience, they would suffer greatly.

This is an essential element for every preacher. Your preaching must contain this element of warning the wayward. Caution them of the devastation that awaits if they travel down the wrong path. Though you may feel uneasy to make such application, it is a necessary part of preaching.

Do you warn your listeners of the danger if they continue to live as they do? Do you admonish them? If you love them, you will.

Urge the Undecided

You must also urge people to pursue the path marked out in Scripture. To be effective, preaching must go beyond instruction to exhortation. To "exhort" (parakaleō) means to call someone to your side. After you teach the mind, you should ignite the heart and summon the will. The idea is to entreat and implore them to follow Christ. You are summoning and pleading with them to respond. It is not enough to merely point out the clearly marked path. You must go further and challenge people to live the word of God in their daily walk.

This urging was seen in Peter's preaching. On the day of Pentecost, he "kept on exhorting them" (Acts 2:40). He pleaded with them to act upon the gospel. Paul would later instruct Timothy, "Until I come, give attention to the public reading of Scripture, to exhortation and teaching" (1 Tim. 4:13). Exhortation is an indispensable component of all authentic preaching. An elder must be "able . . . to exhort in sound doctrine" (Titus 1:9). Paul charged Titus, "These things speak and exhort and reprove with all authority" (2:15).

In the same way, your preaching must be compelling and address not only the mind but also the heart and the will. Beseech and entreat your listeners to respond to the teaching of Scripture. This involves more than stating and explaining the facts. It goes further and pleads with people to act upon what they know to be true.

This kind of passionate appeal must be heard in the preacher's voice and felt in the delivery. As you "exhort" in your teaching, seek to move your hearers to action. Spur them on to pursue the truth you preach and take steps that please God.

Do you exhort those to whom you preach? Do you seek to compel them to respond to the message? Do you plead with them to act upon what they have heard? Do you appeal to them to live for the Lord? If there is no exhortation, there is no true expository preaching.

Persuade the Unconvinced

The word translated "persuasion" (*peithō*) means to prevail upon someone to pursue a course of action. It conveys the idea of winning someone over to believe something and act accordingly in a decisive way. It means to convince by argument, to induce another person to believe. The idea is to move a person to act. You are never to assume a casual, nonchalant approach in the pulpit, nor display a take-it-or-leave-it attitude with your listeners. Instead, seek to move people to believe the truth and live it. Persuasion must be a part of your preaching.

The apostle Paul writes, "Therefore, knowing the fear of the Lord, we persuade men" (2 Cor. 5:11). From this we may reasonably conclude that if there is no persuasion, there is no fear of God in the preacher's heart. Preaching with persuasion is not incidental, but foundational to any effective preaching.

Do you seek to win people to the truth? Do you try to persuade them to pursue the truth?

Comfort the Downcast

Those who preach must also bring comfort to hurting hearts. They must apply Scripture to bring God's peace to discouraged souls. You are to provide encouragement when your listeners are languishing in the valley of despair. Bind up broken hearts that are suffering and lift up the downcast by pouring the healing balm of truth into their open wounds. They are beaten and bruised by the blows of life. Your preaching should offer relief from their stress and anxiety.

Jesus preached by bringing comfort to those downtrodden with life (Ps. 42:3). He encouraged His listeners, "Do not be worried about your life, as to what you will eat or what you will drink; nor for your body, as to what you will put on. Is not life more than food, and the body more than clothing?" (Matt. 6:25). Jesus comforted their troubled souls: "So do not worry about tomorrow; for tomorrow will care for itself. Each day has enough trouble of its own" (v. 34). In His preaching, Jesus sought to ease the heavy burdens of wearied hearts—and so must you.

Jesus set the example for every preacher when He cried out, "Come to Me, all who are weary and heavy-laden, and I will give you rest. Take My yoke upon you and learn from Me, for I am gentle and humble in heart, and you will find rest for your souls. For My yoke is easy and My burden is light" (11:28–30). To those weighed down with the legalism of the Pharisees, Christ called them to come to Him for relief. He models that we must offer comfort to those under the heavy load of trouble.

The apostle Paul gave comfort to those suffering persecution. When he preached in churches he had established, he assured the people, "Through many tribulations we must enter the kingdom of God" (Acts 14:22). These words were intended to encourage disciples that suffering for the kingdom of God is to be expected in following Christ (2 Tim. 3:12). His preaching brought much needed peace to troubled souls. All preaching should console believers that God is with them for their good.

The book of Hebrews is one extended sermon that, among other things, encourages and consoles the persecuted, reminding them of Jesus's reassuring words: "I will never desert you, nor will I ever forsake you" (Heb. 13:5). The result is, "The LORD is my helper, I will not be afraid. What will man do to me?" (v. 6). This exposition brought much needed consolation to their troubled hearts and reaffirmed that Jesus would never desert them in their hour of greatest need.

This same encouragement is what you must give to your listeners. Do you purposefully seek to comfort troubled souls in your preaching? Do you have a sensitive heart toward those who are downcast? Do you provide comfort for people under the heavy blows of life?

Strengthen the Weak

Further, you must strengthen people who are weakening in their faith. Your preaching should seek to bolster them with spiritual fortitude. As you expound the word, you should attempt to uplift their souls. God will use your preaching to embolden fragile saints when they are faltering.

Paul endeavored to build up believers, "strengthening the souls of the disciples, encouraging them to continue in the faith" (Acts 14:22). His preaching was "strengthening" (*epistērizō*) them; that is, making them stronger in their walk with Christ. The apostle's words were a means of imparting sanctifying grace into their lives. By his preaching, he was "strengthening the churches" (v. 41).

Paul assured the elders in Ephesus that "the word of His grace . . . is able to build you up and to give you the inheritance among all those who are sanctified" (20:32). "Build up" (*oikodomeō*) pictures someone building a house to be strong in order to withstand the elements. The preaching of the word fortifies believers with spiritual stamina to undergird them in their faith.

One of your chief goals in preaching must be to embolden your hearers by the exposition of the word. Do you attempt to build up their faith? Do you make it your aim to edify as you seek to convict and challenge? Do you purpose to bolster their spiritual growth?

Equip the Servants

As an expositor, your application must also include equipping believers to serve Christ. The Lord gives gifted leaders to the church—"some as evangelists, and some as pastors and teachers, for the equipping of the saints for the work of service" (Eph. 4:11–12). "Equipping" (*katartismos*) means to restore something that is broken to usefulness. The ministry of the preached word should prepare believers to be effectively used in God's service. Your biblical preaching must train them for ministry in the Lord.

From the pulpit, show people how to study and interpret the Bible and give them the tools to rightly handle the word of truth. You are modeling how to practically apply the Bible to real life, week by week. You are also training people how to apply the word to their lives and how to counsel others.

Your preaching should also equip people in their witness to unbelievers, teaching them the essential truths of the gospel and training them in sharing Christ with their family, friends, and work associates. Under your preaching, they should discover how to refute the many arguments they will hear posed against the gospel. You must train them in bringing unbelievers to the point of decision for Jesus Christ.

Do you model for your congregation various biblical ways to present the gospel? Do you provide them with a defense for the hope that lies within them and tools to study the word for themselves?

Assure the Doubters

In your expositions, you should help people gain the assurance of their salvation. You must aid them in discerning whether they have a right relationship with the Lord. You should preach to help genuine believers gain true assurance of salvation in their hearts. This confidence before God is the result of preaching the gospel with clarity and faithfulness.

An entire book in the Bible, 1 John, is written to give believers assurance: "These things I have written to you who believe in the name of the Son of God, so that you may know that you have eternal life" (1 John 5:13). In this epistle, John gives the necessary evidences of the new birth. He teaches that wherever there is the root of regeneration, there will also be the fruit of sanctification. The root and the fruit are inseparably connected. Eternal life always produces a changed life. Regeneration immediately and inevitably begins the process of sanctification. The assurance of salvation comes, ultimately, through seeing the reality of personal holiness in one's life.

As you preach the evidences of grace, those who hear you will be assured of the genuineness of their relationship with God. Your responsibility is to teach them the marks of true salvation. The distinguishing evidences of a true believer are confessing sin (1:5–10), obedience to the word (2:3–6; 3:24; 5:3), love for the brethren (2:7–11; 3:14–17; 4:7–21), decreasing love for the world (2:15–17), spiritual discernment (2:18–27; 4:1–6), practicing righteousness (2:28–3:10), answered prayers (3:22), and faith in Jesus Christ (3:23; 5:1, 5).

In your expositions, do you address your congregation regarding the legitimate basis for true assurance of their salvation? Do you expose the false evidences upon which to base such assurance? Do you bring the affirmation needed that instills valid confidence of personal conversion?

Awaken the Sleeping

In your preaching, you likewise should awaken those who are spiritually smug and complacent. Many have lapsed into spiritual lethargy. They have been lulled into a deep sleep—a state of unconsciousness toward God. Preaching should be like a trumpet blast that sounds an awakening alarm. It should arouse and capture the attention of spiritually slumbering people. You must disturb them out of their comatose state.

Rather than putting people to sleep, your exposition must awaken them. It should stimulate their minds, enliven their souls, and excite their hearts. Proclaim the truth with fiery zeal. Strong preaching burns its way into the soul of the listener.

The preaching of John the Baptist was described by Jesus as "the lamp that was burning and was shining" (John 5:35). His preaching gave off both light and heat. He was "the voice of one crying in the wilderness" (Matt. 3:3), emitting the light of truth with the fire of passion.

This is how Jesus spoke the word on the road to Emmaus. The two disciples who heard Him responded, "Were not our hearts burning within us while He was speaking to us on the road, while He was explaining the Scriptures to us?" (Luke 24:32). As Jesus explained the word, His words ignited their souls. They were ablaze with excitement for God, and the exposition of the word excited their hearts with a renewed love for Him.

Preaching should enthuse people with new zeal for the kingdom of God. It should raise their affections to live for Jesus Christ. It should set them on fire, and energize them to move forward with renewed vigor to pursue the will of God.

Do your expositions come with a dynamism that arouses slumbering saints who are spiritually lethargic? Does your preaching send a wake-up call to the drowsy in your congregation? Are you mindful of inspiring believers to pursue holiness with greater resolve? Does your preaching come with a motivating force that energizes your listeners to do the will of God?

Challenge the Unaware

Your preaching should call for self-examination, motivating people to search themselves for genuine evidence of saving grace. Paul stresses, "Test yourselves to see if you are in the faith; examine yourselves!" (2 Cor. 13:5). You must ask for honest self-evaluation from your listeners. It is spiritually unhealthy for people to never be challenged to look for fruit in their lives. Preaching must call individuals to inspect themselves and see if God is at work within them.

Jesus often posed questions to cause His listeners to think about where they were spiritually. He asked, "Who do people say that the Son of Man is?" (Matt. 16:13). After His disciples answered, Jesus asked an even more personal question: "But who do you say that I am?" (v. 15). This brought Peter to answer, "You are the Christ, the Son of the living God" (v. 16). Having to answer these probing questions was far more revealing for Peter than if Jesus had told him who He is.

On yet another occasion, Jesus pressed the issue: "For what will it profit a man if he gains the whole world and forfeits his soul? Or what will a man give in exchange for his soul?" (v. 26). These questions were designed to challenge the disciples. The intent was to reveal if they understood what He had taught them and where they were in their spiritual journey.

That Jesus raised these questions in His preaching—and many more—is a model for you to follow. Your pulpit ministry should ask heart-searching questions of those who hear you. This is a key component in making effective application. Your probing questions could be: Where do you stand with the Lord? Have you been converted by His grace? What holds you back from committing your life to Jesus Christ? Is it peer pressure? Is it the sin you would have to abandon? What keeps you from Christ? Why do you hesitate to come to Him? Do you doubt He will receive you?

These questions shift your sermon from the indicative mood—statements of fact—to the interrogative mood. Diagnostic questions cause your listeners to look inward and search for the answers. Piercing questions prompt an audit of one's life. Preaching should cause people to look inward and determine where they are with the Lord. They should take stock of where they stand with Him.

Do you raise questions in your preaching that cause people to examine themselves? Does your preaching regularly call listeners to evaluate their spiritual life? Do you intentionally shift from indicative statements to interrogative questions? Does your pulpit ministry cause individuals to test themselves concerning the state of their soul?

Evangelize the Lost

Making an evangelistic appeal is another essential part of applying the sermon to the listener. Jesus says, "Follow Me, and I will make you fishers of men" (Matt. 4:19). Those called to preach must summon lost people to faith in Christ. After you teach the truths of the gospel, you must make persuasive appeals for them to respond. Evangelizing the lost is mandatory for all who exposit the word.

Consider the preaching of Jesus. He repeatedly urged unbelievers to commit their lives to Him. He called for people to answer His gospel appeals. He commanded His listeners: "Enter through the narrow gate" (7:13). These imperative commands brought people to the place where they must make a critical decision with their life. He cried out, "If anyone is thirsty, let him come to Me and drink" (John 7:37). Through many urgings, Jesus demanded an immediate, decisive response to His gospel invitations.

As Peter and the other apostles proclaimed the gospel, countless souls were won to Christ. Such evangelistic preaching was not an isolated incident but characterized the whole book of Acts. Multitudes were brought to faith in Jesus Christ by the apostles' preaching. To "preach the word," Paul says, you must "do the work of an evangelist" (2 Tim. 4:2, 5). Evangelistic preaching begins with unconverted people within your church. Expositors are charged to be soul winners. Bible preachers must seek to win people to Christ.

This evangelistic fervor must mark your expositions. It is not enough that you teach the truth. You need to also call unconverted listeners to respond to the gospel, which is the power of God unto salvation. They must be "doers of the word, and not merely hearers who delude themselves" (James 1:22). This necessitates that you summon people to respond with saving faith, invite the lost to Christ, and "compel them to come in" (Luke 14:23).

Do you call sinners to believe the gospel? Do you invite them to exercise their will to believe in Christ? Do you ask them to commit their life to Him and compel them to come by faith to Him?

Make the Connection

You must be more than merely right in what you say. You also must be convincing and attempt to secure a favorable decision for Christ from your congregation. Your sermon reaches its high point when the application begins. To be persuasive in preaching is to seek to win over your listeners to the truth. This is a distinguishing mark toward which you must aim when in the pulpit.

In the ultimate sense, only the Holy Spirit can convict and win people to Christ. We, of course, understand that doctrinal truth. But the Spirit works through many means, the primary one being the preaching of the all-powerful word of God. We must be those through whom He works to win the elect to saving faith.

May God use the faithful preaching of His word to bring His chosen ones to Christ—and to Christlikeness.

EIGHT

Improving as a Preacher

ELEVATING THE EXPOSITION

No minister is yet all that he should be.

John MacArthur[1]

To be an effective preacher, you must be ever growing in your abilities in the pulpit, always striving to make progress, no matter how long you have been preaching. Always reach forward to the next level of effectiveness, ever working to improve your proclamation of Scripture.

Your abilities should never remain stationary. Either you are progressing, gaining greater precision and power in the pulpit, or you are regressing. There is no standing still. You are either growing in your gifts as a preacher or reverting. If you are satisfied with where your preaching is, you are surely drifting backward, whether you realize it or not.

Advancing in your pulpit abilities requires not just better techniques, but making headway at a far deeper level. You must develop in both the art and science of preaching. Any progress necessitates more thoroughly mastering the Bible and better understanding the mechanics of preaching. This requires an honest evaluation of where you are as a preacher. Self-awareness is critically important. Know your weaknesses and shortfalls. No one unexpectedly trips and falls upward to higher ground.

It is important to assess where you are as a preacher. You may have years of experience in the pulpit, or you may have only a few years under your belt. You may be better entrenched in the word than your peers, or you may have less Bible knowledge. You may be more spiritually gifted than your colleagues, or you may feel less equipped. Wherever you are, what we will discuss in this chapter will be a help to you.

How can you become more effective in your pulpit ministry? How can you advance to the next level of excellence? How can you have more power in your delivery? The following practical headings provide steps you may take to move forward in your preaching.

Sit under Great Preaching

At the most basic level, learning to preach well is more caught than it is taught. Growth in your skill as a preacher will be significantly enhanced by sitting under other gifted preachers. Careful observations of effective expositors can be even more valuable than being taught in a formal classroom setting. A case can be made that your development as a preacher is most enhanced by consistent exposure to excellent preaching.

When young pastors ask me how they can become better preachers, I always encourage them to sit under the best preaching they can find. I urge them to sit near the front of the worship center and glean as much as they can, up close, from the delivery of a gifted expositor.

You will learn more in person than listening remotely through an electronic device. If you are a young, aspiring preacher, you need to be present in a church service to best observe and experience what constitutes great preaching. In that close proximity, you will be more likely to sense the emotion of the preacher, as well as the gravity, pathos, and nonverbal communication.

If you are already preaching, you should attend conferences where noted preachers are speaking. Search for these opportunities. You can greatly sharpen your skills by sitting under their preaching. When there is more than one speaker at a conference, it is helpful to compare one speaker to another. Observe their strengths and weaknesses and relate them to where you are in your preaching.

You can contrast similarities and differences in styles of preaching and study what makes one preacher's methods more effective than another. Observe their body language, gestures, and use of eye contact. Not everything you detect will be something you will incorporate. You must remain yourself, but you can learn much from them.

Listen to Great Preaching

If you cannot sit under great preaching in person, you can still learn through electronic means. Avail yourself of audio and video sermon recordings. This technology is useful in learning to preach better. When you watch or listen to gifted expositors, try to recognize what contributes to their excellence. Some of these qualities can be things you implement in your preaching.

Tune your ear to the sound of notable preaching. Listen to both the tone and tempo of an effective delivery, to the pace and pitch of the voice. Hear the preacher alternate speaking faster then slower, louder then softer. You can absorb these speaking dynamics.

Sermons are primarily meant to be heard, not read. It is not merely *what* the preacher says that matters, but *how* it is said. The manner of delivery can either enhance receptivity to the message—or hinder it. How a pastor comes across to listeners is vitally important to the success of the sermon. This is why you need to *listen* to effective preaching. It will teach you the vocal patterns that make a sermon work effectively.

Read Great Preaching

You can also learn much from studying great preaching in print, either in a book or online. Reading enables you to easily see the structure of a sermon's various parts.

In my seminary years, I learned little about how to construct a sermon from my classroom instruction, even though my professor wrote one of the most highly regarded textbooks on expository preaching. Helpful as it was, I learned far more from reading the sermons of pulpit giants from past centuries such as Jonathan Edwards, George Whitefield, and Charles Spurgeon. As I surveyed each page, I saw the role played by each element of the sermon: introduction, main headings, subheadings, cross-references, extrabiblical quotations, illustrations, emphatic statements, and closing appeal.

The written sermons of these giants can also teach us how to present the gospel and make an evangelistic appeal. We can see how they called sinners to faith in Jesus Christ. In print, I have learned from George Whitefield and Charles Spurgeon how to preach the gospel and urge lost souls to believe in the Savior. Through their sermons, I learned the manner to call the unconverted to repentance and faith.

I have also learned much from reading sermons of our modern era. Reading the expositions of James Montgomery Boice, the late pastor of Tenth Presbyterian Church in Philadelphia, Pennsylvania, is like taking a master class in preaching. Before entering the pastorate, Boice was an English major at Harvard University, and he served as editor of *Christianity Today.*

Among his many strengths, Boice exercised a masterful command of the English language. He also possessed a remarkable skill in asking diagnostic questions that probed the minds and hearts of his listeners. I also learned from Boice the value of using church history to support a truth, and he modeled for me the use of systematic theology in the pulpit.

Transcribe Great Preaching

Another discipline in improving your preaching is transcribing an expository sermon. This meticulous exercise allows you to learn the internal workings of a biblical sermon. The hands-on interaction of taking down the words of a uniquely gifted preacher gives penetrating insight into what makes a sermon work. Such a ground zero involvement with an exposition is an important exercise in learning its essential components.

As a young preacher, I listened to much preaching on cassette tapes. I would hit the play button, listen to ten seconds, and then stop it in order to write down what the preacher said. Then I would hit the play button for another ten seconds, stop it, and write the next words down. It would take hours for me to transcribe a sermon. But through this tedious process, I grasped the essential parts of an excellent sermon.

As I transcribed great preaching, I began to recognize what I needed to incorporate into my preaching. These examples showed me what an effective sermon looked and sounded like. By taking notes, I learned firsthand what great preaching was like. I could see a well-crafted sermon in my own handwriting. I absorbed the movement, flow, and cadence of great sermons that shaped my understanding of what I needed to do. This may also help you.

Learn from Several Preachers

Do not limit yourself by being influenced by only one pulpit personality. Such a myopic focus will likely restrict your development. Having only one example could set a low ceiling over your preaching. You will adopt not only that preacher's strengths, but also their weaknesses. Hearing multiple preachers will ensure the balance you need in learning to preach.

Every preacher has blind spots in their pulpit ministry. You will be best served if you surround yourself with a variety of examples as you learn to find your own voice. Each positive example can add something you need to your understanding of preaching. Each will round off some of your rough edges. Set before you multiple models as you develop your own approach to preaching. Each will make a unique contribution in completing your skill set.

In my early years of preaching, I learned by sitting in church under two legendary Baptist preachers, Adrian Rogers and W. A. Criswell. Their bold preaching put a fire in my bones that still burns to this day. I was then influenced up close by two Presbyterian preachers, James Montgomery Boice and R. C. Sproul. I gleaned much from these powerful preachers' theological brilliance and linguistic precision. Finally, two Independent preachers left an indelible mark on me: S. Lewis Johnson and John MacArthur. From these two, I learned exegetically grounded, sequential exposition through books of the Bible.

I needed the particular strengths of each of these six preachers to sharpen me. Each had a solid commitment to Scripture, though they were unique in their approaches to the pulpit. Each had their own forte that developed different aspects of my preaching. Through their diverse influences, I became a more well-rounded preacher. Looking back, if I had been affected by only one of these pastors, I would have been limited in my growth.

Preach as Much as Possible

Ultimately, the chief way to learn to preach is to actually do it. As you cannot learn to ride a bike while sitting in a classroom, but have to go outside and physically pedal, the same is true in preaching. You must stand in a pulpit before real people with an open Bible and preach. I want to urge you to take the initiative to seek out more speaking opportunities in order to increase your effectiveness. Even speaking to a small group will give you much-needed experience. Seize as many opportunities as you can to proclaim the word.

The trajectory and tone of your preaching will be altered to fit each specific gathering. Each of these preaching opportunities will enhance a different aspect of your delivery. Each setting makes a unique contribution to elevating your skills; a diversity of venues will help round you out as a preacher.

You need to preach regularly to become more proficient, just as the more you practice the piano or golf, the more likely you are to become a better player. The same is true in preaching. You need to preach as much as you can to advance to the next level. More preaching leads you to learn better sermon preparation and delivery.

When I was a young pastor, I began a regular pattern of preaching on Sunday mornings, Sunday evenings, and Wednesday evenings. In addition, I taught a weekly men's Bible study, plus Sunday school, for many years. That came to a total of five preparations per week for thirty-four years. I also preached at different conferences and special meetings.

Such a constant, rigorous preaching routine kept me grounded in the Bible. It also taught me how to use my language tools, Bible commentaries, and other resources well. Repeated preaching helped me learn how to best arrange my notes and use them most efficiently in the pulpit.

Preach in Different Settings

You will be best served by preaching in as many different settings as you can. Preaching two sermons in two different places is better than preaching one sermon two times in the same place. The different sightlines, pulpits, faces, and responses will bring different things out of you.

This does not mean you must travel around the country to learn how to preach. You simply need to find various preaching venues in your own church or city. Each setting will require a different delivery from you, which will expand your expositional abilities. Otherwise, your preaching may settle into a predictable rut and fail to develop well. There can be a monotony about preaching in only one particular place that can easily lead you to fall into one-dimensional repetition in your delivery.

Preach a Short Book

If you are new to preaching, you should consider choosing a shorter book in the Bible to learn how to preach. Perhaps you recently graduated from seminary and are entering your first pastorate. If you do not have much experience with expository preaching, a book with fewer chapters may be easier for you.

A short epistle can be a wise place to begin. These apostolic letters of tightly worded truth are easier to preach for new expositors. James Boice, for example, began his pulpit ministry by preaching verse by verse through Philippians, a book with only four chapters. John MacArthur started his pastorate at Grace Community Church by preaching sequentially through the six chapters of Ephesians.

After I graduated from seminary, I started my first pastorate by expositing Colossians, a letter of only four chapters. I began there because it was a brief book that I could more easily handle. A longer book would have overwhelmed me. I needed to start in a book with fewer chapters and work my way up to a book with more chapters.

A book like Ruth or Jonah could also be a good place to begin to get your feet on the ground. Or you could start with Titus or Jude.

Preach the Whole Bible

It takes preaching the whole Bible to make a whole preacher. One tendency we can have as preachers is to camp out in our favorite section of Scripture. Or we can settle into those books that are easiest to expound. For most young preachers, this means the shorter epistles. But we must learn to preach from every portion of Scripture.

I certainly began in the comfort zone of one part of the Bible early in my ministry. But to develop as a preacher, I knew I needed to stretch myself and exposit other genres of Scripture. Learning to preach narratives was essential for my growth. By preaching the stories of the Bible, a didactic preacher will likely become a more interesting preacher. Instead of you falling into the trap of giving a dry lecture, this difficult genre of the great stories in the Bible could infuse energy and interest into your pulpit presentation. When you preach narratives, you will no longer have the bland tone of a cognitive lecturer. Instead, expositing these dramatic stories will help you become more impassioned.

Preaching a story in Scripture usually requires a higher energy level. There is a movement that flows from its rising action, internal conflict, and striking conclusion. I learned to tap into this excitement when I first preached the narrative portions of the Gospel of John. What further grew me was preaching through the book of Psalms. The exposition of these worship songs—from lament and praise psalms to trust and imprecatory psalms—ushered me into greater dimensions of preaching.

Improve Your Grammar

As you preach in the pulpit, your use of proper grammar matters. Bad grammar draws attention to itself. Misuse of the English language will reflect poorly on the preacher and leaves a negative impression with listeners. Improper grammar can cause people to focus on your linguistic flaws rather than the truth you are preaching. In fact, it can even discredit you with some of your listeners. They may wonder if your preaching content is as inaccurate as your grammar.

When I graduated from seminary, my grammar needed serious improvement. In my first pastorate, some retired English teachers in my congregation would write down my grammatical mistakes during the sermon. After the service, they would pull me aside in the lobby and hand me their lists. It was painful for me, like receiving a report card every Sunday.

These interactions initially bothered me, but the Lord used them to prepare me for future ministry in places where my grammar mattered even more. These post-sermon encounters taught me to care about a better use of the English language. This, in turn, helped me to gain a hearing with some congregants that I would not have had otherwise.

Ask a family member or trusted friend to correct you when they hear you use incorrect grammar. Their feedback will bring you a world of good. Have an elder or mentor make a list of grammatical mistakes they hear in your preaching. There is no better way to extract bad grammar from your teaching than to hear from someone who loves you enough to tell you about it. Thank them when they correct you. I must warn you that they will have to do this repeatedly until you can consciously correct your poor habits.

Read, Write, and Rewrite

If you want to speak with powerful sentences—excellent cadence, diverse length, strong lead-in phrases, dramatic emphasis, and better word choice—you can learn this skill by reading great literature. Observe how literary giants craft sentences and diversify their vocabulary. Note how they use figures of speech and analogies. As you detect masterful ways of communicating, a better use of words will be absorbed into your preaching delivery.

When writing your sermon manuscript, compose it as though you can hear yourself preaching. Consider reading each sentence aloud, so you can track the flow of your message. C. S. Lewis once said great writers write with their ears, not with their eyes. Do not write your sermon notes as though you were submitting them to a seminary professor for a term paper or research project. Instead, write with the dynamic energy of the spoken word, as though you can hear yourself preaching.

You must also learn to edit what you write. There are no great writers, only great rewriters. Few preachers are gifted enough to sit down and write a sermon manuscript without the need to return and amend what they have written. Rewriting your sermon notes is an important part of the process as you strive for excellence in how you communicate the truth of God's word.

Important parts of rewriting involve better word choices, simpler sentence structure, and more colorful expressions. If writing makes you accurate, rewriting sharpens you to be more precise. It also helps you trim down what you have written to not be unnecessarily wordy. Editing your writing helps you speak better in the pulpit.

Read Books on Preaching

You will also enhance your skill in expository preaching by reading books about it. These books can sharpen your perspective about what constitutes authentic preaching. They will help clarify your thinking about the essential parts of an expository sermon, and give you better insight into what makes your sermon work—and what hinders your message.

In my estimation, the one book on preaching you most need to read is Martyn Lloyd-Jones's *Preaching and Preachers*, which was originally given as a series of lectures at Westminster Theological Seminary. Lloyd-Jones edited these addresses into the individual chapters of this book. Another excellent title is *Preaching: How to Preach Biblically* by John MacArthur and the faculty at The Master's Seminary, which will enlighten you in the technical aspects of exposition.

Additionally, J. W. Alexander's *Thoughts on Preaching* is as timeless as when he first wrote it in the nineteenth century. Other vital resources include *Evangelical Eloquence* by R. L. Dabney, *Between Two Worlds* by John Stott, and *Lectures to My Students* by Charles Spurgeon. All of these books are must-reads for expositors and can upgrade pulpit ministries.

Reading the biographies of great preachers is also helpful, and you will find these books to be both instructional and inspiring. I strongly recommend the two-volume biography *George Whitefield* by Arnold Dallimore, which will make you want to preach. *The Forgotten Spurgeon* by Iain Murray will move you to stand strong when you preach in the face of opposition. The two-volume biography of Martyn Lloyd-Jones by Iain Murray, *D. Martyn Lloyd-Jones*, will elevate your view of the ministry, especially preaching. Reading works like these will make a world of difference in your pulpit ministry.

Read about Church History

Reading church history will also improve your preaching. Before I attended seminary, I did not know much about the church at large in past centuries. My church history classes opened a whole new world for me, and much of it involved the lives of preachers. I learned about the great preachers of the Reformation and the Puritan Age. I studied the powerful preachers of the Great Awakening, the Modern Missionary Movement, and the Great Victorian Era. The dynamic movements of these eras challenged me to have a greater desire to be used by God.

Though I was centuries removed from the preachers of these times, I experienced a close fellowship with them. I felt like I was being personally discipled by them and being challenged by their legacies. Through the study of church history, I learned that there is always a high price to pay to preach the word, involving sacrifice and suffering.

I once preached in a Bible conference with the president of the seminary from which I received my master's degree.

He was a skilled theologian and gifted lecturer, though not known as a preacher. First he preached, then I did. Following the last evening of our sessions, he said to me, "One thing is certain. *We* did not teach you how to preach." Though this may sound like a criticism, he meant it as a compliment. He recognized my skill was not gained from our school's classrooms but instead largely learned from past masters of the pulpit, from stalwarts like the Reformers, the Puritans, Whitefield, and Spurgeon.

Read about the Martyrs

A sobering part of church history that inspires greater faithfulness is the martyrs. You should read and learn about the lives of these saved men and women who gave their lives for the advancement of the gospel. The accounts of these valiant people will implant steel into your backbone as you preach. Heroic figures inspire heroic preaching.

In one of his resolutions, Jonathan Edwards purposed to think much about the martyrs: "10. Resolved, when I feel pain, to think of the pain of martyrdom, and of hell."[2] He understood the strength to be drawn from studying these heroes. Read about the price that William Tyndale paid unto death for translating the Bible into English. Remember such enormous sacrifices when you stand to preach the word. It will help nail your flag to the mast and your feet to the floor.

In the front flyleaf of my preaching Bible, I have taped a picture of John Rogers. He was burned at the stake in Smithfield, London, on February 4, 1555. He will be long remembered as the first martyr put to death by Queen Mary I of England, whom history remembers as Bloody Mary. How can I not strive to preach better when brave men like him have gone before me?

Rogers's crime was finishing Tyndale's work of translating the Bible into the English language. In addition, Rogers preached against the Roman Catholic Mass and proclaimed salvation by faith in Christ alone. For this, he was publicly martyred before the startled eyes of his wife, eleven children, and congregation. In comparison, any criticism I have ever received for my preaching is nothing. When you read church history, you see your difficulties in the right perspective.

Read about other English Reformers like Hugh Latimer and Nicholas Ridley, who were burned at the same stake in Oxford for their unwavering allegiance to the true gospel. While strapped to the stake, Latimer said, "Play the man, Master Ridley. We shall this day light such a candle by God's grace in England, as I trust will never be put out."[3] Read about Thomas Cranmer plunging his right hand into the flames before being martyred. In a moment of weakness, he had previously signed a recanting of his confession of faith in the true gospel. That right hand suffered destruction first because it had compromised first.

These heroic accounts will surely embolden you with deeper conviction and greater courage as you preach the word.

Be Zealous for God

If you are to preach with spiritual power, you must be zealous for the glory of God. To be effective in the pulpit is to be consumed with the majesty of His name. The more you love God, the better you will preach His word. Do not let anything quench your passion for His kingdom. Boring sermons generally come from bored preachers.

It is critically important to maintain a holy passion for God. For this to occur, you must live in His word, and His word must "richly dwell within you" (Col. 3:16). Commune with God in prayer. Adore His greatness. Confess all known sin. Be quick to repent. Trust Him explicitly. Magnify His name. Extol His greatness. Long for His fellowship. As you live and serve out of a growing love for Him, your preaching will be taken to another level.

After Jesus's resurrection, He appeared to two disciples on the road to Emmaus (Luke 24:13–21). After "He explained to them the things concerning Himself in all the Scriptures" (v. 27) and then left them, they responded, "Were not our hearts burning within us while He was speaking to us on the road, while He was explaining the Scriptures to us?" (v. 32). Ask God to do this same heart-igniting work within you. This is a prayer God will surely delight to answer. A fire in the pulpit begins with you catching fire in the Bible. It will soon spread to the pews.

Be Spirit-Filled

The empowering of the Holy Spirit is absolutely essential in preaching. The same Spirit who inspired the Scriptures must anoint preachers today to preach the Good News to those afflicted by sin (Isa. 61:1). If we are to preach with spiritual power, we must be dominated by the Holy Spirit, as we discussed in the latter half of chapter 3. A review of those pages may be helpful for you. There is no substitute for His powerful work in our lives as we proclaim the word.

In the book of Acts, whenever believers were filled with the Spirit, they spoke with boldness. Jesus had promised the disciples, "You will receive power when the Holy Spirit has come upon you; and you shall be My witnesses both in Jerusalem, and in all Judea and Samaria, and even to the remotest part of the earth" (Acts 1:8). They were supernaturally energized to preach throughout the book of Acts (2:4; 4:8, 31; 6:3, 5; 7:55; 8:17; 9:17; 11:15; 13:9, 52).

Strive for Excellence

No matter where you are in your pulpit ministry, you should always strive toward greater excellence. Whether you have been preaching for one year or fifty years, always be reaching forward to progress to the next level of effectiveness. Such advancement requires hard work, involving many of the suggestions I have recommended to you in this chapter. If it were easy to improve your preaching, you would already be there.

The apostle Paul challenged the Thessalonians to "excel still more" (1 Thess. 4:1). Though his words pertained to their Christian walk, they also apply to each one of us who preach. We *must* excel still more.

NINE

In Pursuit of Holiness

DISCIPLINING THE LIFE

A minister may fill his pews, his communion roll, [and] the mouths of the public, but what that minister is on his knees in secret before God Almighty, that he is and no more.

John Owen[1]

As we reach our final pages, let me stress again the vital truth that the purity of the messenger affects the impact of the message. Power in the pulpit starts with the integrity of the preacher. Nothing can be more important than the minister's pursuit of holiness. God must prepare the preacher before the preacher can prepare the message.

Robert Murray M'Cheyne, a young pastor in nineteenth-century Scotland, showed such an extraordinary zeal for

God that to this day he continues to challenge preachers to pursue holiness. This noted minister saw himself as an instrument in the hand of the sovereign God, one set apart to proclaim His word. The effectiveness of his ministry, he realized, was largely dependent on the purity of his life.

Writing to a missionary preparing for the mission field, M'Cheyne stressed that he must not neglect his own holiness. To make his point, M'Cheyne used the analogy of a soldier advancing into battle:

> How diligently the cavalry officer keeps his saber clean and sharp. Every stain he rubs off with the greatest care. Remember, you are God's sword—His instrument. . . . In great measure, according to the purity and perfection of the instrument will be its success.[2]

Rightly did M'Cheyne understand that God's messenger is like a sword that must be kept morally clean to be effective in ministry and must be pure in order to be spiritually sharp in the Master's use.

Great Likeness to Jesus

In this same letter, M'Cheyne explained, "It is not great talents God blesses so much as great likeness to Jesus. A holy minister is an awful weapon in the hand of God."[3] He uses the word *awful* to mean that which is terrifying to the Enemy. Only a holy preacher can inflict a devastating blow to the forces of darkness. The power of any minister is largely dependent on the purity of his inner life.

Before M'Cheyne died at age twenty-nine, he concluded that the greatest need of his people was his own personal holiness. He understood that the quality of his pulpit ministry depended on his personal godliness. There could be no contradiction between his personal life and the effectiveness of his ministry. Consequently, M'Cheyne prayed for himself, "Lord, make me as holy as a pardoned sinner can be."[4]

This priority to pursue personal holiness must be our determined aim. The strongest preachers are those with an inseparable connection between the purity of their lives and the power of God upon their pulpit ministries.

If you have been called by God to preach, your personal godliness is of utmost importance. If you have a career as an accountant, builder, or dentist, your personal life would not be so central. But the fact that you have been summoned by a holy God to preach His word places upon you a greater responsibility. This high call demands a holy life. You must model the message you preach.

While no preacher is sinless, it is nevertheless mandatory they be morally upright. Paul writes that preachers must be "above reproach" (1 Tim. 3:2). There must be no area marred by habitual sin. Their personal character is the most important platform from which they speak. Their integrity is foundational to their ministry.

Discipline Yourself for Godliness

To address this more carefully, I want us to consider Paul's first pastoral epistle to Timothy. In this letter, the apostle underscores the extreme importance of Timothy disciplining himself for the purpose of godliness. Paul writes,

In pointing out these things to the brethren, you will be a good servant of Christ Jesus, constantly nourished on the words of the faith and of the sound doctrine which you have been following. But have nothing to do with worldly fables fit only for old women. On the other hand, discipline yourself for the purpose of godliness; for bodily discipline is only of little profit, but godliness is profitable for all things, since it holds promise for the present life and also for the life to come. It is a trustworthy statement deserving full acceptance. For it is for this we labor and strive, because we have fixed our hope on the living God, who is the Savior of all men, especially of believers. (1 Tim. 4:6–10)

At the time of Paul's writing, Timothy was serving as pastor in Ephesus, at a church established by the apostle Paul himself. A false teaching known as gnosticism threatened the spiritual stability of the church (1:3–11). Some women were overstepping their bounds in the church and teaching men with authority (2:9–15). Unqualified men were serving as elders (3:1–7), because the church had laid hands on them too hastily (5:22). They also had unqualified deacons active in the church (3:8–13). Widows in the congregation had great needs that were being overlooked (5:3–16).

Amid this turmoil, Paul charges Timothy, first and foremost, to maintain the spiritual condition of his soul as he steps forward in ministry.

Your greatest need as a preacher is your personal godliness. The truth you proclaim must be modeled in your own life. Before you preach to others, you must preach to yourself. In short, you must practice what you preach. Otherwise, you will forfeit divine power in the pulpit—or maybe even become disqualified.

Feast on the Word

Paul begins by exhorting Timothy to be a "good servant of Christ Jesus . . . nourished on the words of the faith and of the sound doctrine" (4:6). In serving others, he must expose the many lies confronting the believers. As he fends off false teachers, Timothy must maintain a steady diet of Scripture. His continual feeding upon the word is essential to his own spiritual health and ministry.

Timothy must be "nourished" (*entrephō*) on the truths of the word, which means to be brought up, or trained, in sound doctrine. This pictures him being educated in the Scripture that can nurture his soul. The present tense requires that this be a continuing growth in the Scripture. This spiritual food consists of "the words of the faith," which is Paul's description of the whole body of truth in Scripture. The definite article "the" identifies this as the objective "faith"—the full purpose of God revealed in Scripture.

Timothy must continue to nourish his soul on the teaching contained in "sound doctrine." This refers to teaching about God, humankind, salvation, and holiness. The word translated "sound" (*kalos*) means beautiful, excellent, and good. "Doctrine" (*didaskalia*) means teaching or instruction. This instruction is perfect because it has come from God. It is absolutely true because "it is impossible for God to lie" (Heb. 6:18).

Charles H. Spurgeon exemplified the same devotion to the word:

> It is blessed to eat into the very soul of the Bible until, at last, you come to talk in Scriptural language, and your very style

is fashioned upon Scripture models, and what is better still, your spirit is flavored with the words of the Lord.[5]

Every preacher must be immersed in the whole Bible until it permeates their entire being. Their personal Bible reading and study, along with their sermon preparation, should overflow into the lives of the congregation. As they are in the word of God, the word will soon be in their listeners.

German Reformer Martin Luther was mightily used because he was such an ardent student of the word of God. Luther wrote,

> For some years now, I have read through the Bible twice every year. If you picture the Bible to be a mighty tree and every word a little branch, I have shaken every one of these branches because I wanted to know what it was and what it meant.[6]

This explains the power Luther wielded as he stood to preach. Martyn Lloyd-Jones echoes the same truth: a preacher must be dedicated to a regular reading of Scripture.

> Do not read the Bible to find texts for sermons, read it because it is the food that God has provided for your soul, because it is the word of God, because it is the means whereby you can get to know God. Read it because it is the bread of life, the manna provided for your soul's nourishment and well-being.[7]

John Stott also prioritized the importance of the preacher being saturated with the word: "Because the Christian pastor is primarily called to the ministry of the word, the study of

Scripture is one of his foremost responsibilities."[8] A pastor's knowledge of God's word must be comprehensive. Affirming that every preacher should possess a command of the Scripture, Stott stated:

> The systematic preaching of the word is impossible without the systematic study of it. It will not be enough to skim through a few verses in daily Bible reading, nor to study a passage only when we have to preach from it. No. We must daily soak ourselves in the Scriptures. We must not just study, as through a microscope, the linguistic minutiae of few verses, but take our telescope and scan the wide expanses of God's word, assimilating its grand theme of divine sovereignty in the redemption of mankind.[9]

Follow the Truth

Paul acknowledges Timothy's pursuit of Christ by saying, "You have been following" (1 Tim. 4:6) the words and teaching of Scripture. "Following" (*parakoloutheō*) means to conform to someone's beliefs or practice by paying special attention to someone else. Paul acknowledges that Timothy has been pursuing the truth in his daily walk. What he has learned with his mind, he is living with his life. The truth was saturating his soul and affecting the way he conducted himself in all his life.

"Following" the truth is absolutely critical if you are called to preach. You must embody the message you preach as a living epistle of what you teach. You should be able to say, "I exhort you, be imitators of me" (1 Cor. 4:16). Your life should be worthy of imitation by your listeners as you follow Christ. Jesus said, "A pupil . . . after he has been fully trained, will be like his teacher" (Luke 6:40). Your congregation will soon follow your example. You must practice what you preach *before* and *after* you preach.

Forsake the Lies

Paul next adds this admonition: "But have nothing to do with worldly fables fit only for old women" (1 Tim. 4:7). Timothy must refuse all worldly lies that have no basis in the truth. The imperative command is an ardent rejection of such error (*paraiteomai*), which means to decline, refuse, and reject these lies. He must not entertain these corrupt errors, because they will defile his mind. Rather, he must set his mind upon what is true and pure (Phil. 4:8).

"Worldly fables" refer to vain imaginations from fallen and darkened minds. They originate from "deceitful spirits" who conceive "doctrines of demons" (1 Tim. 4:1). These fables are "worldly" (*bebēlos*), indicating they are poisoned and profane. Preachers are to reject this filthy foolishness and assign no credibility to it. It has no place in any sermon.

Paul had already condemned these wicked lies when he wrote, "Pay [no] attention to myths and endless genealogies, which give rise to mere speculation" (1:4). People of God must refuse all fanciful stories that do not originate in the word. "Genealogies" refer to allegorical and speculative uses of Old Testament accounts involving family trees. Whatever is not taught in Scripture must be rejected and not brought into the pulpit. These strange teachings are full of the devil's deadly venom and are the product of carnal minds that deal in trash, not the truth. Paul again mentions these "myths" as what unconverted people crave (2 Tim. 4:4).

Resist Men's Commandments

Paul issued this same warning to Titus; he must resist "Jewish myths and commandments of men who turn away from the truth" (Titus 1:14). These people were fabricating teachings from the Old Testament by adding worldly perversions to them that were fanciful, untrue, and deceptive. Such damnable lies are often used as license for immoral behavior. Once the authority of Scripture is compromised, illicit lifestyles are sure to follow.

This is a needed word for preachers today because many falsehoods come disguised in the name of true spirituality. However, they only promote unbridled carnality. This deadly poison comes with many different labels. It is contained in many forms, whether it be incredulous liberalism or social agendas that seek to better people apart from preaching the gospel. Mysticism and unfounded political conspiracy theories also threaten to dominate the pulpit. True discernment is required to distinguish between the true and the false.

There are many deceptive fallacies that compete for the minds of naïve pastors. Secular ideologies influence pastors today as never before. Unwarranted speculations that take the place of straightforward instruction from Scripture should have no place in any preacher's mind. Neither should they be allowed in the pulpit.

Face the Discipline

In light of these encroaching dangers, Paul charges Timothy: "Discipline yourself for the purpose of godliness" (1 Tim. 4:7). Advancement in godliness requires self-discipline. All successful ministry starts with the disciplined spiritual life of the minister. When there is personal discipline in the preacher, it will lead to spiritual growth in the pews. Again, as Jesus said, "Everyone, after he has been fully trained, will be like his teacher" (Luke 6:40). In this case, the congregation will become like Timothy as he disciplines himself.

Spiritual Fitness Required

The verb translated "discipline yourself" (*gymnazō*) is drawn from athletic imagery and comes into our English language as "gymnasium," which is a place to train or undergo discipline. Athletes would go into a gymnasium and strip down so no clothing would restrict the extension of their limbs. This freedom of movement would allow them to expend maximum effort in training to build up their muscles. Paul is saying that Timothy must be like those athletes who undergo strict discipline.

Any competitor serious about winning must enter the gymnasium consistently and undergo regimented workouts. Even so, Timothy must align his heart and life according to the word of God. He must "lay aside every encumbrance and the sin which so easily entangles [him]" (Heb. 12:1). If need be, he must deny himself certain Christian liberties for the sake of his preaching ministry. He must remove all excess baggage that holds him back from being at prime effectiveness.

Timothy must work out in the word and labor in prayer. He must exercise his spiritual muscles in obedience. He must shed the excess fat of self-centeredness. Paul exemplified, "I discipline my body and make it my slave, so that, after I have preached to others, I myself will not be disqualified" (1 Cor. 9:27). If he is to have power in preaching, Timothy cannot be passive about this, but must take charge of his spiritual life.

The same is true for you as a preacher today. If you are to excel at the highest level in the pulpit, you must discipline yourself spiritually. Work up a spiritual sweat in the word and through repentance. Tone your spiritual muscles in prayer. Monitor your heart rate for God in worship. Do heavy lifting in learning sound doctrine. Beat down your fleshly desires. Build up your endurance by meditating on Scripture.

Personal Godliness Mandated

The chief aim of spiritual discipline, Paul says, is "for the purpose of godliness." The word "godliness" (*eusebeia*) comes from a Greek root word that carries the idea of devoutness and piety. It refers to the inner condition of Timothy's heart for God. He must be gripped with a proper fear of God. Paul writes elsewhere that believers must work out their salvation in "fear and trembling" (Phil. 2:12). A growth in grace is never realized casually or flippantly, never with a lighthearted attitude. Godliness requires a sober reverence for God that takes Him very seriously. No ministry can advance beyond one's personal awe for God.

Charles H. Spurgeon sought to establish this same priority in his own life. When he addressed the students in his Pastor's College, he urged these young preachers in training:

It will be in vain for me to stock my library, or organize societies, or project schemes, if I neglect the culture of myself . . . for books and agencies, and systems, are only remotely the instruments of my holy calling . . . my own spirit, soul, and body, are my nearest machinery for sacred service; my spiritual faculties and my inner life, are my battle axe and weapons of war.[10]

Spurgeon concluded that any loss of purity would guarantee a loss of power in the pulpit. He reasoned that the preacher's spiritual life was far more important than his books.

Such godliness is nonnegotiable for every preacher. Who we *are* is more important than what we *do*. Our godliness is more important than our giftedness, our purity than our preaching, and our maturity than our ministry. What we are before God takes precedence over what we do before people. How we live is more important than how we labor. Our walk with God is more important than our work for God.

Foresee the Reward

As a master teacher, Paul paints a vivid picture in Timothy's mind by extending this illustration of bodily discipline to spiritual discipline. He compares the two by saying, "For bodily discipline is only of little profit, but godliness is profitable for all things" (1 Tim. 4:8).

In the first century, winning athletes were placed on a high pedestal by admiring spectators. Statues of these figures chiseled out of marble lined the streets leading into major cities. Aspiring young men were dedicated to excelling at the highest level of competition. They were not halfhearted in their training but poured themselves into the discipline required to be a world-class athlete. Their sole ambition was attaining the victor's crown. These champions would be granted tax-exempt status and receive free education. Flowers would be tossed at their feet as they walked the streets.

Amid this body-glorifying culture, Paul concedes that there is "little" (*oligos*) gain in physical training. While there is a relatively small profit, there is, nevertheless, some gain to it. However, the profit from bodily discipline is short-lived, lasting only for a brief season. But the benefits of spiritual discipline will last for eternity. Physical training builds up the body, but spiritual discipline strengthens the soul. Physical training is limited because it is only for this life. However, spiritual discipline is unlimited because it affects eternity.

Paul adds, "But godliness is profitable for all things" (v. 8), indicating that spiritual discipline develops godliness, which is far more profitable. The meaning of "profitable" (*ōphelimos*) indicates what is useful, beneficial, advantageous. Spiritual training in the word and prayer will be invaluable for his personal holiness. The point is that discipline is necessary for greater growth in Christlikeness.

But conversely, if there is little training in spiritual matters, there will be little progress in godliness. An undisciplined life hinders growth. There is no easy path for Timothy—or any preacher—to model the message they preach.

When Paul affirms that spiritual discipline is profitable "for all things," he is recognizing its value in every area of life. In contrast to the "little" benefit from physical training, the advantage of spiritual discipline extends to "all [*panta*] things." "All" literally pertains to the totality of Timothy's life. Spiritual discipline yields great gain in the whole person—mentally, emotionally, relationally, socially, and ministerially.

What high motivation this is to study God's word and meditate upon it. We should be challenged to resist temptation, exercise self-control, and do all things necessary to be in top spiritual shape.

To be spiritually disciplined "for the present life" brings joy, happiness, spiritual power, and blessing now—but "also for the life to come" (v. 8), referring to eternal reward. The athlete who competes according to the rules will stand at the judge's seat and receive a victor's reward (2 Tim. 2:5), and the same is true in our spiritual lives. Disciplining ourselves will lead to running life's race well and will result in great joy when we stand before the Lord. As we grow in godliness, there will be greater recognition and reward in "the life to come" (*mellousēs*), or in the future, forever with God.

Fix Your Hope

Finally, Paul underscores the extreme significance of what he has asserted. There must be no doubt in Timothy's mind regarding its importance, and Paul therefore emphasizes this to his young son in the faith—and to every preacher today.

The apostle begins, "It is a trustworthy statement deserving full acceptance" (v. 9). "A trustworthy statement" (*pistos logos*) stresses the great importance of what he is saying (1 Tim. 1:15; 3:1; 2 Tim. 2:11; Titus 3:8). This statement is "deserving full acceptance" (1 Tim. 4:9), meaning Timothy must not only agree with it but embrace it.

The faithful words are found in the previous two verses: "bodily discipline is only of little profit, but godliness is profitable for all things" (v. 8), and "discipline yourself for . . . godliness" (v. 7). If Timothy is to progress in his sanctification, he must be like a champion athlete and enter into strict training. He must buffet his body under a strict regimen (1 Cor. 9:25–27) and keep the rules laid out by God (2 Tim. 2:5).

To this end, Paul charges Timothy: "It is for this we labor and strive, because we have fixed our hope on the living God, who is the Savior of all men, especially of believers" (v. 10). If he is to grow spiritually in greater conformity to Christ, Timothy must expend great energy in self-discipline.

To "labor" (*kopiaō*) means to become weary or tired; it conveys the idea of exerting oneself physically, mentally, or spiritually until there is nothing left to give. It means to work hard, even to toil. Paul applies the same word to the ministry of preaching (1 Tim. 5:17). This is how Timothy must resist sin and obey the word of God. He must strive to obey the truth with every fiber of his being.

To "strive" (*agōnizomai*) means to fight, struggle, or engage in a contest. This pictures a wrestler in a tough match and a runner in a grueling marathon. It is also used to describe a soldier fighting in a war against a formidable foe. Timothy must agonize against sin in his pursuit of godliness.

These two verbs, *labor* and *strive*, are in the present tense, indicating these are continuous requirements. Timothy must always be laboring and striving against the flesh within him. Further, the devil is always prowling about like a roaring lion, seeking someone to devour (1 Pet. 5:8). Timothy cannot let his guard down for one moment.

He must have "fixed [his] hope on the living God" (1 Tim. 4:10). This "hope" (*elpizō*) means a certain confidence that something will come to pass.[11] It is this "fixed hope"—a steadfast and unwavering assurance about the future—that enables Timothy to look ahead to when God will conform him into the image of Christ. This confidence in God will motivate and empower him to keep pursuing holiness.

The strong motivation for self-discipline is fueled by this hope in God. Timothy must trust the "living" (*zōnti*) God as he preaches to a dying world. Therefore, God is the only hope for the salvation for "all men" (v. 10), that is, all those who believe in Christ Jesus. With this fixed hope, Timothy is to proclaim the gift of eternal life that is in Jesus Christ, who is the only Savior for the world—specifically, for all those who trust Him.[12]

This future hope in God should generate spiritual energy within every preacher. On the last day, every herald of truth will appear before the judgment seat of Christ (2 Cor. 5:10). Those who have disciplined themselves and lived according to the rules (2 Tim. 2:5) will be recognized by the Judge for eternal reward. As a preacher of the gospel, you must push yourself to excel. You must know that one day you will stand before the Lord Jesus Christ, and He will reward you for your faithfulness in the word.

"I Have Been before God"

One noted minister who sought to discipline himself for the purpose of godliness was the renowned Colonial Puritan preacher of the eighteenth century, Jonathan Edwards. He was arguably the greatest preacher ever born on American soil. At eighteen and nineteen years of age, Edwards wrote seventy resolutions that would serve as a moral compass for his spiritual life. He read these purpose statements as a means of staying on track in his pursuit of Christlikeness as he sought to live every day as though it were the last day of his life. In this effort, he was determined to discipline himself in the use of his time, tongue, and talents.

On January 14, 1723, Edwards wrote resolution sixty-three: "On the supposition that there never was to be but one individual in the world at any one time who was properly a complete Christian."[13] He reasoned there must be one person at any one moment in time who is regarded by God to be the greatest Christian alive. This one person most embodies the virtues of the Lord Jesus Christ.

With this goal fixed in his gaze, Edwards wrote, "Resolved: I will act just as I would do if I strove with all of my might to be that one who should live in my time."[14] It was by no accident that this nineteen-year-old young man, then serving as an intern pastor on Wall Street in downtown New York, would become America's greatest pastor, preacher, philosopher, theologian, and author. Edwards had set a course for his life: that he would glorify God by striving to gladly exhibit Christ in his generation.

Two days earlier, on January 12, 1723, Jonathan Edwards wrote in his diary of his commitment to live for God, not for himself.

I have been before God, and have given myself, all that I am and have, to God; so that I am not, in any respect, my own. I can challenge no right [to] this understanding, this will, these affections, which are in me. Neither have I any right to this body, or any of its members—no right to this tongue, these hands, these feet; no right to these senses, these eyes, these ears, this smell, or this taste. I have given myself clear away, and have not retained anything as my own. I have been this morning to Him, and told Him, that I gave myself wholly to Him. I have this morning told Him that I did take Him for my whole portion, looking on nothing else as any part of my happiness, nor acting as if it were; and His law, for the constant rule of my obedience; and would fight with all my might against the world, the flesh, and the devil, to the end of my life; and that I did believe in Jesus Christ, and did receive Him as a Prince and Saviour; and that I would adhere to the faith and obedience of the gospel, however hazardous and difficult the confession and practice of it may be. Now, henceforth, I am not to act, in any respect as my own.[15]

As Edwards charged himself, so you are charged today by Paul's words to Timothy to "discipline yourself for the purpose of godliness" (1 Tim. 4:7). If you are to be a preacher, you must labor and strive to work out your salvation in fear and trembling. Resist temptation and put to death the deeds of the flesh. Pursue holiness, without which no one shall see the Lord. Forget what lies behind and press forward to what lies ahead. Discipline yourself like a world-class athlete and bring your whole life under the control and the mastery of the Lord Jesus Christ.

As you consider your calling to proclaim the word, remember that God uses the instruments He makes holy. May God sanctify you in every area of your life as you hold forth His holy word.

A FINAL CHARGE TO PREACHERS

UPHOLDING THE WORD

As a preacher, you stand at a critical crossroads. Two divergent paths lay before you. Which way will you go? Will you follow the path clearly marked in Scripture? Will you preach as God directs in His word? Or will you choose to travel the way of compromise? Will you preach as worldly pressures would shape you into their mold? You must decide.

The Pulpit of the Broad Path

To the left lies the broad path. It is the way most traveled in the ministry. It is easily accessed and requires no sense of calling to enter. It allows very little study to advance on it. In fact, many who enter here rely on others, whether through plagiarism or a "preaching team." The way is so wide that it allows any theology to be taught. It is far and away the most popular and appealing road in ministry. Larger crowds may attend it. It is light on Bible content but heavy on personality and charisma. This route is more about style than substance. It is a wide-open thoroughfare that attracts many preachers.

This pulpit avoids the controversial subjects taught in the Bible. It preaches only those truths that people want to hear. It gives plenty of illustrations and applications but no doctrine or admonition. It makes no demands upon those who sit under it.

This is the pulpit of the broad path. Tragically, it leads its listeners down the broad road. It panders to the fleshly appetites of its many travelers. It amuses them to death. It fills the building with people but leaves the pulpit devoid of truth. This is the ear tickling about which Paul warns (2 Tim. 4:3). In the end, this kind of preaching leads to the destruction of many.

The Pulpit of the Narrow Path

To the right is the narrow path. It is the way less traveled in the ministry. Few preachers choose it. You must be called to enter it. Its message is narrowly defined in what it teaches and what it requires. It has guardrails on each side that allow for no deviation.

Far fewer travelers choose to follow this way. Its pulpit focuses upon the purity of the message, not the popularity of the preacher. This road is built with gold, silver, and precious stones, not wood, hay, and straw.

The preacher in this pulpit proclaims the full counsel of God. On this narrow road, every hard truth is expounded.

Every command is issued. Every sin is exposed. Every grace is extended. It is not fixated on redeeming the culture but rather aims at redeeming sinners.

On this route, the pulpit expounds both divine sovereignty and human responsibility. It teaches both heaven and hell. It calls for both repentance and faith. It is often met with resistance and persecution. Few preachers are prepared to pay this price.

Throughout the centuries, the preachers who have been mightily used by God have been faithful heralds of the cross of Jesus Christ. There are no exceptions to this.

Which path have *you* chosen to follow? Every preacher must decide which road to take. The broad path of shallow, superficial Christianity? Or the narrow path of authentic discipleship under the sovereign lordship of Jesus Christ?

On the last day, when you stand before the Lord, may you be found faithful—and may you hear His divine approval: "Well done, good and faithful slave" (Matt. 25:21).

ACKNOWLEDGMENTS

The book has been greatly enhanced by several people, each of whom I want to thank.

Carissa Early, my editor at OnePassion Ministries, invested much time in editing and improving this manuscript. Her contribution was invaluable to this project.

Brian Fairchild was a great help with many technical details in this work.

John Sloan provided valuable feedback on this book's content.

Lindsey Spoolstra, my project editor for Baker Books, saw this book through its many stages.

Stephanie Duncan Smith, senior editor for Baker Books, also helped in the final manuscript.

NOTES

Chapter 1 Divinely Summoned

1. Thomas Watson, *The Beatitudes* (repr., Edinburgh: Banner of Truth Trust, 2000), 21.

2. D. Martyn Lloyd-Jones, *Preaching and Preachers: 40th Anniversary Edition* (Grand Rapids: Zondervan, 2011), 17.

3. Lloyd-Jones, *Preaching and Preachers*, 17.

4. Fred W. Meuser, *Luther the Preacher* (Minneapolis: Augsburg Publishing House, 1983), 39.

5. Charles H. Spurgeon, *C. H. Spurgeon Autobiography: The Early Years*, vol. 1 (Edinburgh: Banner of Truth Trust, 1962), 185.

6. Iain Murray, *D. Martyn Lloyd-Jones: The First Forty Years, 1899–1939* (Edinburgh: Banner of Truth Trust, 1982), 80.

7. Lloyd-Jones, *Preaching and Preachers*, 118.

8. Arnold Dallimore, *George Whitefield: The Life and Times of the Great Evangelist of the 18th Century Revival*, vol. 1 (Edinburgh: Banner of Truth Trust, 1970), 82–83.

9. Marion Harland, *John Knox* (New York: G. P. Putnam's Sons, 1900), 16.

10. Spurgeon, *C. H. Spurgeon Autobiography*, 196–97.

11. Spurgeon, *C. H. Spurgeon Autobiography*, 197.

12. Lloyd-Jones, *Preaching and Preachers*, 117.

13. Murray, *D. Martyn Lloyd-Jones*, 94–95.

14. Lloyd-Jones, *Preaching and Preachers*, 116.

15. Lloyd-Jones, *Preaching and Preachers*, 116–17.

16. Murray, *D. Martyn Lloyd-Jones*, 93.

Chapter 2 The Preacher's Mandate

1. Martin Luther, as cited in John Blanchard, comp., *More Gathered Gold: A Treasury of Quotations for Christians* (Hertfordshire, England: Evangelical Press, 1986), 243.

2. R. Albert Mohler, *He Is Not Silent: Preaching in a Postmodern World* (Chicago: Moody, 2008), 73.

3. Mohler, *He Is Not Silent*, 73.

4. Gustav Friedrich, s.v. "kerygma," *Theological Dictionary of the New Testament* (Grand Rapids: Eerdmans, 1964), 687–88.

5. Walter C. Kaiser Jr., "A Call to Renew the Work of God," commencement address, Dallas Theological Seminary, April 29, 2000.

6. Martin Luther, *Luther's Works: Sermons 1*, vol. 51, ed. John W. Doberstein (Philadelphia: Fortress, 1959), 77.

Chapter 3 Behold Your God

1. Sinclair Ferguson, *Feed My Sheep: A Passionate Plea for Preaching* (Orlando, FL: Reformation Trust, 2008), 104.

2. John Piper, *Expository Exultation: Christian Preaching as Worship* (Wheaton: Crossway, 2018), 16.

3. Lloyd-Jones, *Preaching and Preachers*, 110.

4. Lloyd-Jones, *Preaching and Preachers*, 110.

5. Lloyd-Jones, *Preaching and Preachers*, 72.

6. Cotton Mather, *Student and Preacher: Or Directions for a Candidate of the Ministry* (London: Charles Dilly, 1781), 4.

7. Martin Luther, *The Bondage of the Will*, trans. J. I. Packer and O. R. Johnston (repr., Grand Rapids: Baker Academic, 2012), 71.

8. Martin Luther, *The Cambridge Companion to Martin Luther*, ed. Donald K. McKim (Cambridge: Cambridge University Press, 2003), 138.

9. Martin Luther, *Luther's Works: Table Talk*, vol. 54, ed. Theodore G. Tappert (St. Louis: Concordia, 1955), 74.

10. Charles H. Spurgeon, *The Metropolitan Tabernacle Pulpit*, vol. 7 (Pasadena, TX: Pilgrim Publications, 1977), 169.

11. Charles H. Spurgeon, "Christ the Glory of His People," in *The Metropolitan Tabernacle Pulpit Sermons*, vol. 14 (London: Passmore & Alabaster, 1868), 467.

12. Lloyd-Jones, *Preaching and Preachers*, 322.

13. R. C. Sproul, "The Whole Man," in *The Preacher and Preaching*, ed. Samuel T. Logan Jr. (Phillipsburg, NJ: P&R Publishing, 1986), 113.

14. John Knox, *The History of the Reformation of Religion Within the Realm of Scotland* (London: Adam and Charles Black, 1898), 40.

15. Charles Spurgeon, as cited in John Stott, *Between Two Worlds: The Art of Preaching in the Twentieth Century* (Downers Grove, IL: InterVarsity, 1982), 334.

Chapter 4 In the Study

1. John Piper, *The Legacy of Sovereign Joy* (Wheaton: Crossway, 2000), 68.

Chapter 5 Preparing Your Exposition

1. Stuart Olyott, *Preaching: Pure and Simple* (Bryntirion, Wales: Bryntirion Press, 2007), 75.
2. Lloyd-Jones, *Preaching and Preachers*, 76.
3. Jonathan Edwards, *The Works of Jonathan Edwards*, vol. 1 (repr., Edinburgh: Banner of Trust, 2005), 391.

Chapter 6 Stepping into the Pulpit

1. Charles H. Spurgeon, *The Metropolitan Tabernacle Pulpit*, vol. 59 (Pasadena, TX: Pilgrim Publications, 1979), 82.
2. John Flavel, *The Character of an Evangelical Pastor, Drawn by Christ* (London: T. Rutt Shacklewell, 1814), 15.
3. J. C. Ryle, *Luke*, ed. Alister McGrath and J. I. Packer (Wheaton: Crossway, 1997), 29.
4. James Montgomery Boice, sermon delivered at Bible Church of Little Rock, Little Rock, AR, n.d.
5. J. I. Packer, "Introduction," in Logan, *The Preacher and Preaching*, 11.
6. Philip Ryken, *Preach the Word, Essays on Expository Preaching: In Honor of R. Kent Hughes*, ed. Leland Ryken and Todd Wilson (Wheaton: Crossway, 2007), 200.
7. William Perkins, *The Works of William Perkins*, vol. 2 (Grand Rapids: Reformation Heritage Books, 2015), 148.
8. John MacArthur, *Preaching: How to Preach Biblically* (Nashville: Thomas Nelson, 2005), 265.
9. J. C. Ryle, *Simplicity in Preaching* (Edinburgh: Banner of Truth Trust, 2010), 4.
10. James Usher, as quoted in Ryle, *Simplicity in Preaching*, 5.
11. MacArthur, *Preaching*, 265.
12. Walter C. Kaiser Jr., *Toward an Exegetical Theology: Biblical Exegesis for Preaching and Teaching* (Grand Rapids: Baker Books, 1981), 239.
13. Kaiser, *Toward an Exegetical Theology*, 239.
14. Theodore Beza, as quoted in Leroy Nixon, *John Calvin, Expository Preacher* (Grand Rapids: Eerdmans, 1950), 31.

15. Richard Baxter, *The Autobiography of Richard Baxter* (London: J. M. Dent & Sons, 1925), 381.

16. C. H. Spurgeon, *The Metropolitan Tabernacle Pulpit*, vol. 23 (Pasadena, TX: Pilgrim Publications, 1967), 698.

17. Stott, *Between Two Worlds*, 275.

18. Richard Baxter, as quoted in Charles Bridges, *The Christian Ministry* (repr., Edinburgh: Banner of Truth Trust, 2018), 318.

19. Lloyd-Jones, *Preaching and Preachers*, 104–5.

20. Phillips Brooks, *Lectures on Preaching Delivered Before the Divinity School of Yale College in January and February, 1877* (New York: E. P. Dutton and Company, 1877), 8.

21. Lloyd-Jones, *Preaching and Preachers*, 279.

Chapter 7 Making It Personal

1. Daniel Webster, as cited in John A. Broadus, *On the Preparation and Delivery of Sermons* (repr., Birmingham, AL: Solid Ground Christian Books, 2005), 245.

Chapter 8 Improving as a Preacher

1. John MacArthur, *The MacArthur New Testament Commentary: 1 Timothy* (Chicago: Moody, 1995), 180.

2. Jonathan Edwards, "The Resolutions of Jonathan Edwards," accessed July 29, 2021, http://www.jonathan-edwards.org/Resolutions.html.

3. John Foxe, *Foxe's Book of Martyrs* (Philadelphia: E. Claxton & Co., 1881), 250.

Chapter 9 In Pursuit of Holiness

1. John Owen, as cited in I. D. E. Thomas, *A Puritan Golden Treasury* (Edinburgh: Banner of Truth Trust, 1977), 192.

2. Andrew Bonar, *Memoir and Remains of the Rev. Robert Murray M'Cheyne* (repr., Edinburgh: Banner of Truth Trust, 2009), 282.

3. Bonar, *Memoir and Remains*, 282.

4. Bonar, *Memoir and Remains*, 159.

5. Charles H. Spurgeon, *The Autobiography of Charles H. Spurgeon*, vol. 4 (Chicago: Fleming H. Revell, 1900), 268.

6. Luther, *Luther's Works: Table Talk*, 165.

7. Lloyd-Jones, *Preaching and Preachers*, 184.

8. Stott, *Between Two Worlds*, 181.

9. John Stott, *The Preacher's Portrait* (Grand Rapids: Eerdmans, 1961), 30–31.

10. C. H. Spurgeon, *Lectures to My Students* (Edinburgh: Banner of Truth Trust, 2011), 2.

11. The English rendering "fixed our hope" is translated from the single Greek verb *ēlpikamen*. This verb is perfect, active, and indicative, demonstrating the completed, or "fixed," nature of the "hope."

12. The word translated "all" (*panta*) can have a range of meanings: some of all groups, all of some groups, or all of all groups. "All" in this context would mean, then, some of all groups in the world. Among all people groups in the world, Christ is the only Savior (see Acts 4:12).

13. As cited in William S. Morris, *The Young Jonathan Edwards: A Reconstruction* (Eugene, OR: Wipf & Stock, 2005), 203.

14. Jonathan Edwards, *The Works of President Edwards*, vol. 1 (New York: S. Converse, 1829), 72.

15. Jonathan Edwards, *A Treatise Concerning Religious Affections* (Philadelphia: James Crissy, 1821), xiv.

Dr. Steven J. Lawson is founder and president of OnePassion Ministries, a ministry designed to equip a new generation of Bible expositors and to spread the message of God's word around the world. The focus of Dr. Lawson's ministry is the verse-by-verse exposition of Scripture and training others to do the same. He is the author of over thirty books, including *Show Me Your Glory*, *New Life in Christ*, *The Moment of Truth*, *Foundations of Grace*, *Pillars of Grace*, *The Unwavering Resolve of Jonathan Edwards*, *The Expository Genius of John Calvin*, and many more.

Dr. Lawson is a teaching fellow with Ligonier Ministries, professor of preaching and dean of the Doctor of Ministry program at The Master's Seminary, and executive editor for *Expositor* magazine. He is also on the boards of Ligonier Ministries and Reformation Bible College. A graduate of Texas Tech University (BBA), Dallas Theological Seminary (ThM), and Reformed Theological Seminary (DMin), he has served as a pastor for thirty-four years and presently lives in Dallas, Texas, where he teaches *Steadfast Hope* and *The Bible Study*.

ONEPASSION

For God. For His Glory. Forever.

**OnePassion Ministries exists to
ignite a supreme passion for God and His glory in
all people throughout the world.**

Head to **onepassion.org** for
Bible studies, sermons, blogs, and more resources.

What actually happens when you trust Christ for salvation?

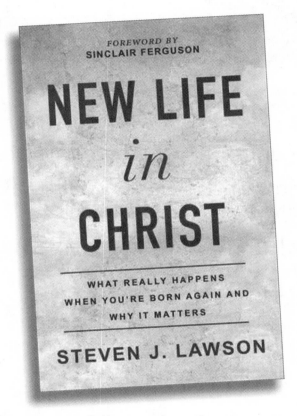

Steven Lawson carefully examines the encounter between Jesus and Nicodemus found in John 3 to uncover the nature of this spiritual rebirth. He shows you the necessity of the new birth, how God changes our hearts through it, and what follows after, from baptism and involvement in a local church to handling doubts and setbacks.